COMMON SENSE FOR A PROSPEROUS LIFE

BOOK 3

THE ENTRY-LEVEL CEO

Simple Secrets to Build a Profitable Business
(Even with No Experience!)

Mark Ashe

THE ENTRY-LEVEL CEO © 2022, 2026
by Mark Ashe. All rights reserved.

Published by Author Academy Elite
PO Box 43, Powell, OH 43065
www.AuthorAcademyElite.com

All rights reserved. This book contains material protected under international and federal copyright laws and treaties. Any unauthorized reproduction, distribution, transmission, display, or use of this material is prohibited.

No part of this book may be reproduced or transmitted in any form or by any means, electronic or mechanical, including photocopying, recording, scanning, scraping, or by any information storage and retrieval system, without the express prior written permission of the author.

Without limiting the author's exclusive rights under copyright law, no part of this work may be reproduced, copied, extracted, scraped, ingested, analyzed, or used for the purpose of training, fine-tuning, developing, or improving artificial intelligence systems, machine learning models, or generative models—whether commercial or non-commercial—without the author's prior written consent.

The author expressly reserves all rights to license this work for any AI-related uses.

Identifiers:

LCCN: 2020922145

ISBN: 978-1-64746-601-5 (paperback)
ISBN: 978-1-64746-602-2 (hardback)
ISBN: 978-1-64746-603-9 (ebook)

Available in paperback, hardback, e-book

Scripture quotations are taken from the Holy Bible, New Living Translation, copyright ©1996, 2004, 2015 by Tyndale House Foundation. Used by permission of Tyndale House Publishers, a Division of Tyndale House Ministries, Carol Stream, Illinois 60188. All rights reserved.

Cover designs by
Perry Yeldham, 21Thirteen Design, Inc.
perry@21thirteen.com
and
George Foster, Foster Covers

Other Books by Mark Ashe

The *Common Sense for a Prosperous Life* series

Riches Beyond the Bling
Invest Like a Wealth Manager
Unchain Your Brain
Private Choices, Public Power

Whatever you can do, or dream you can, begin it.
Boldness has genius, power, and magic in it.
—Johann Wolfgang von Goethe

CONTENTS

Author's Notes ix

Chapter 1—Step Into The Current 1
Chapter 2—Increasing Your Income 6
    Where to Start 7
    Building a Business. 10
    What Determines Success? 12
    The Number One Mistake 14
Chapter 3—Ten Business Guidelines 19
    1. Hire The Best 20
    2. Train Thoroughly 23
    3. Monitor Employee Performance 28
    4. Establish Rules That Protect Fluidity. . . . 31
    5. Teach Everyone To Run Toward Problems. . 32
    6. Make Everything "Disney Quality" 33
    7. Avoid Problematic Customers 36

  8. Do Not Take Work Without Enough Profit 37

  9. Keep A Financial Safety Margin 37

  10. Apply The Golden Rule 40

Chapter 4—The 80/20 Rule 46
  The Problem of Pricing. 46

  Outgo Matters, Too 49

  You Have to Make a Real Profit 50

Chapter 5—Shrewdness In Business 54
  Don't Be a Patsy. 55

  Beware the Unsolicited Contact 60

  Get Legal Advice Before Making Any Commitment. 63

  Use the Best Professionals. 65

  Never Buy During the Glitter Show 66

  Three More Ways to Be Shrewd 68

Chapter 6—Do You Have A Desire To Work For Yourself? 71
  Let's Recap. 71

  Do You Have What It Takes? 75

  The Call. 78

Appendix—Did These Ideas Cross Your Mind? 80
        Investing in Real Estate 80

        What About Stocks?. 81

        Invent and Market a Product or Create
        Intellectual Property. 83

        Ideas Require that You Take Action. 85

About The Author. 89

AUTHOR'S NOTES

As I sit in my study, I am looking at a framed photograph of Orison Swett Marden. Mr. Marden wrote a lot in the late 1800s about character and its relationship to wealth. He was orphaned as a young boy and put out to hard labor as little more than a slave. Overworked and underfed, he was often beaten by a tyrannical master. Half-starving most of the time, he would sneak an extra bite of food when he found it, terrified of the beating he would receive if he were caught. With no one to aid him, encourage him, guide him—or even love him—he yet *lifted himself* to become one of the preeminent authors of his time. He wrote with authority on the subject of rising from limiting circumstances to achieve a satisfying place in life.

After submitting his first book, *Pushing to the Front,* to several publishers—unsure if any would be willing to print it—to his surprise, publishers actually fought each other over the rights to the book. That book was reprinted again and again and distributed around the globe! Governments bought the book for nationwide distribution in their schools.

THE ENTRY-LEVEL CEO

In a later book, *Good Manners: A Passport to Success*, Mr. Marden penned twenty-seven words that set the course of my adult life:

> ***It is the duty of every young person, and especially of every young man, to set about the task of becoming financially independent. The amount is inconsequential.***

From the first time I read those words, now thirty-five years ago, those two sentences became my personal philosophy—and my obsession. They became my life's field manual and I began a passionate pursuit to attain financial independence.

Even though I still am not a financial sophisticate or a business tycoon (or even had those things as goals), by the age of forty-five I lived on a beautiful farm in the foothills of the North Georgia mountains and I was debt-free and financially independent. My wife and children were living a blessed life, and I was there with them to enjoy every day of it.

Armies issue their new soldiers a "field manual." When faced with a decision, a soldier can go to the manual, refer to the appropriate section, and see quickly what to avoid and what course of action to take to increase the odds of a desirable outcome. I have long been of the opinion that if a practical reference manual could be written for making the major decisions of life—especially if written in an engaging style—a great need would be met for us civilians fighting the battles of life.

To that end, I have written the Common Sense for a Prosperous Life book series, five quick-read handbooks that cut straight to the heart of the most important issues of life:

1. earning and spending,
2. saving and investing,
3. running a business,

4. creative thinking, intention and focus, and
5. mature judgment, marriage, and other personal choices.

But I chose to write these books—including the one you now hold in your hand—with great reluctance. Here's how it happened.

In 2008 I witnessed the global financial meltdown that would shake the world's markets for years, but I had seen it coming. Almost all of the "prosperity" everyone seemed to be enjoying leading up to the crash was an illusion built on excessive debt and other bad decisions.

During those earlier years of society-wide excessive borrowing and spending, an unbidden idea kept pushing itself up, forcing its way into my mind. The thought seemed preposterous, an errant notion passing through the wrong mind, and, at first, I treated it exactly like that. Over time, however, it grew into a conviction that I could not escape, even as I continued to thrust it away.

Here is that thought:

Mark, you write a book that will give the reader a healthy foundation for decisions concerning money, business, and personal life. This current foolishness—the "You can get rich quick and live rich now; here's how!" mantra being fed to the unsophisticated and gullible public by new money magazines, how-I-got-rich authors, and breathless news anchors on financial channels excitedly reporting the day's Wall Street winners—must be confronted.

The healthy intention to become an independent, balanced, self-restrained adult has been lost. Independence, not consumption, must once again be held up for all to see as the proper purpose of labor. You are to write a book that will spell out, in simple terms, a practical mindset toward money, business, and life that will provide a road map to help ordinary men and women see clearly to make wiser choices.

As I have said, I repeatedly dismissed this most unwelcome impulse. After many years of hard work in my own business, I had no appetite for such a time-consuming task, nor did I feel competent. Not only did I feel unqualified to write about these things—after all, my accomplishments are modest when compared to those of the wealthy best-selling authors so prevalent on bookshelves—but I did not believe I had any gift at all for writing, on *any* subject. I did not want, nor have I ever desired, to write a book.

For several years, I continued to consider the thought ridiculous. Then I had a health scare that turned out to be a false alarm. But this was the turning point for me. Why? Because the first thought that went through my mind when I feared bad news was not for myself or my family. To my shock, it was instead, "I should have written that book."

That's when I realized this work was something I *must* do, I was *intended* to do, whether or not I thought it reasonable. And even before I returned the call to the doctor's office, I made up my mind that I would begin.

In 2010—after nearly a decade of my hard work—*Your Money & Your Life: A Guide to Building Character and Capital* was published. The feedback I got was that it was fantastic, but so varied in topics and filled with good information that it would've been helpful to be more subject-specific.

So, I went back to work for a few more years, and now you have in your hand the result—one volume in a five-book series called *Common Sense for a Prosperous Life*. One way or another, the writing of these books has taken much of my time for nearly eighteen years, and, at this moment, I still have no idea if this series will ever see the light of day. But I do know this much: books such as these are needed *badly*, and if these books are ever published everyone who reads them

AUTHOR'S NOTES

will be better off because they will finish each book with far greater clarity of thought for making decisions well that will determine the quality of their life.

Only a fortunate few are born into this world with a "wealth consciousness"—a mind that expects or creates wealth—or gifted with a highly marketable talent. The rest of us have to devote a great deal of our time to earning money and deciding how our very limited resources should be used. The *Common Sense for a Prosperous Life* series was written to give just this sort of reader a mature and sensible mindset toward all kinds of money matters, and also a blueprint for conquering our private demons and making personal choices that are as clear as "Follow the yellow brick road."

Let me begin by stating the obvious. For all but the truly wealthy, building a comfortable life will require several things:

- You must handle whatever you earn deliberately, so it does not slip away.

- You must earn more money than is required for food, clothing, shelter, and other living expenses (which, I admit, is increasingly difficult to do).

- You must not be careless with the money you save.

- You must overcome your own internal hindrances.

- You must not forfeit your progress to an undisciplined private life.

By the time you have finished reading this series, you will have a road map for the five "musts" above.

Book 1—*Riches Beyond the Bling: Clear Thinking on Money, Financial Independence and Life's True Riches* reveals how to handle the money you earn, purposefully.

Book 2—*Invest Like a Wealth Manager: Simplify Your Thinking to Invest Your Money with Confidence* gives you my own common-sense guidelines for saving and investing.

Book 3—*The Entry-Level CEO: Simple Secrets to Build a Profitable Business (Even with No Experience!)* is ideal for those with a desire to work for themselves. It relates some thoughts on increasing your income by building a business of your own.

Book 4—*Unchain Your Brain: Move Beyond Fear and Discouragement and Start Living with Purpose* delivers a powerful read for overcoming fear and discouragement and moving you toward your next goal.

Book 5—*Private Choices, Public Power: Personal Decisions that Determine Your Destiny*, the fifth and final book in the series, is filled with practical help regarding personal issues, which, if handled carelessly, can wreck a life.

None of these books is a sermon, and they are not boring—I promise. I believe every page will grip you with its practical and immediate common sense. Pick up any of the books, open them anywhere, read three pages, and I trust you will not want to quit reading from right where you are. To my mind, that is the test of a well-written and worthy book: there is no place in it that does not quickly engage the reader on a personal level.

The lessons contained within are timeless. They will be just as helpful to a reader sixty years from now as today. So, if you are a parent and you can read this book without considering it imperative to set aside a copy for each of your children, I have

AUTHOR'S NOTES

failed. If you are a wife and you can read this book without insisting that your husband also read it, I have failed.

I truly believe you will not toss these aside: I am *that* confident that the five books in the *Common Sense for a Prosperous Life* series have no substitute in the marketplace. Having read hundreds of such books myself, I believe these are among those rare works immediately useful to every reader in every generation.

Welcome into my major life assignment, my best effort to make the world a better place by giving the reader practical instruction for the most important issues of life.

Choose well and prosper.

Mark Ashe
Gainesville, Georgia
2020

CHAPTER 1
STEP INTO THE CURRENT

People that do nothing get less than nothing; they go backwards. Stagnant water kills. Moving water has life.

—Tracy Ashe

There is honor and dignity in honestly won financial independence that no amount of financed luxury cars, furnishings, or impressive homes can compensate for. When a man or woman can live standing on his or her own two feet, without fawning for favors and without cringing before anyone else's decisions concerning their future, he or she has accomplished something of real, lasting value. I believe that the honorable attainment of a reasonable level of personal independence is a *primary responsibility* of every healthy person and should be given a position of first importance from the beginning of active life, far above our preferences for material things.

Over the years, I have been alarmed by how few people think this way. My misgivings became reality with the financial meltdown of 2007–2008 affecting the world's banks, businesses, stock markets, and real estate—a recession which proved to be long term and deep, affecting almost every home in every country in the developed world—with almost no one ready for it.

Years before the events of 2007–2008 actually occurred, I saw trouble coming. Almost all the "prosperity" I saw, both in corporate America and in the lives of my acquaintances, was an illusion created by a toxic brew of debt. With few exceptions, everyone I knew was living beyond his or her means.

Governments were spending borrowed money at reckless levels. Our financial institutions were leveraging profits with billions of dollars' worth of inscrutable derivative contracts, many of which were interrelated in ways that few understood. Artificially low-interest rates—a product of the Federal Reserve Bank's refusing to allow a much-needed correction in the economy—combined with congressional lawmakers' encouraging government-insured lenders to make home loans to unqualified buyers, were producing irresponsible balance sheets on both sides of the deal, for banks and homeowners.

Instead of holding these highly questionable loans, the lenders worked with Wall Street's masters of illusion to package and hawk them to unsuspecting institutional investors as "solid mortgage-backed securities." As a result, there was a temporary flush of cheap credit for buying homes available even to the most unworthy of borrowers. An equally euphoric real estate bubble replaced the recently deflated stock market bubble, which had imploded in 2000.

And the lessons of that stock market debacle were quickly forgotten with the new wave of "prosperity."

Homeowners were feeling rich and taking loans against their ever more valuable homes to support spending, which, in reality, they could not afford. To my way of thinking, too much depended on nothing going wrong. America's homeowners, banks, brokerage firms, and businesses were highly leveraged, and all were, as the saying goes, "dancing on a volcano."

STEP INTO THE CURRENT

Despite the euphoria, I did not feel good about what I saw. In this headlong rush to live wealthy, the chance to live well was being lost.

Yes, I could see trouble coming, and I knew I was in a race to get out of the way before the house of cards fell. I made it, with a few years to spare. How? By stepping into the current and becoming—through hard work and much trial and error—an entry-level CEO.

Stepping into the Current

My stepfather, Frank Echols, was a truck driver for Johnson Motor Lines. In 1961, he started a part-time business roofing homes. His goal was to make an extra $100 a month. I would not recommend roofing as a business, but the story of how he began has instructive value regarding the subject of stepping into the current.

As a truck driver, Frank often delivered roofing shingles. One day when he was making a delivery, he asked a roofer at the jobsite if he was making any money. The man, Coley Cater, said he made a few hundred extra dollars a month. Frank asked Mr. Cater if he would install roofing for him. Coley said he would. Frank then asked Coley to come by his house and look at his home and give him the price for putting a new roof on it. That was all the knowledge he had of the roofing business.

> If your goal to build a better life does not affect how you spend a portion of your time every day, then you don't have a goal.

Yet, a few evenings later, Frank went through his neighborhood telling neighbors he was going into the roofing business, handing them a business card that read simply, "Echols Roofing." A neighbor asked Frank to give him a price for roofing his house. Frank looked at the house and, as he told me later, "It looked just a little bigger than the house I lived in. So, I added $50 to the price Coley had given me for replacing my own roof. My neighbor told me to go ahead, and when the job was done I had made $100. I was in business!"

Frank worked at his new trade in the evenings and on weekends, and the business grew modestly. Fifteen years later, when Johnson Motor Lines was suddenly shut down, thousands of workers found themselves past fifty years of age with no job. By then, Frank could support himself with his income from Echols Roofing. A modest side business would have been a strong buffer for the other suddenly unemployed men and women.

I am now going to give you the most important sentence you will ever read regarding how to earn more money:

*The only way to learn how to do
what you do not yet know how to do
is to do it.*

You have to learn by doing. There is no such thing as starting after you know what to do. Learning comes from *doing*. If you have an idea for a business, take a step toward it every day. Just *do something* every day to bring it closer to reality. If your goal to build a better life does not affect how you spend a portion of your time every day, then you don't have a goal. Reading my book series is a great start. My life's work is intended to connect you with your life's purpose.

My wife Tracy and I were vacationing last week at the beautiful Phoenician Resort in Scottsdale, Arizona. While we were relaxing at the pool, I shared with her the mixed emotions I felt when writing about this subject, knowing that most people have no idea how to get started with their ideas. Tracy's response was so immediate, emphatic, and (typically) insightful that I thought, "How can this be a dilemma? There is only one answer to that question, and it is the same for everyone."

STEP INTO THE CURRENT

She said,

Things start with an idea. Then you write it down and just start doing something toward it every day, even when you don't see a way, and, eventually, a few years later, you look back and you'll have done it! That's what we did.

Individuals who really want to change their circumstances don't let what they do not yet know stop them from stepping into the current, even if only in small steps. A larger place in the world does not come from wanting or thinking or talking or planning or praying or sending someone a "faith seed offering." It comes from what you *do* every day that is different from what the average person chooses to do with his or her time. That is why I require of myself that at least one hour of every day be spent doing something that at least has the potential to change my future for the better.

That is why for seven years I read instructive books every day—even though I detested reading—and kept at it until it was a habit. That is why I went to work in a line of business that was not to my liking, but was the only thing I could see to do at the time. That is why I persisted for years despite discouragement, all the while praying for a way forward. That is why I refused to go back to being a policeman, which I enjoyed, even when my business seemed more like a punishment for my foolish ambition.

Why? Because, whether I liked it or not, what I was doing for twelve hours a day at least had the potential to make my future better.

So as long as I was earning enough to get by on, I was going to stay where at least it *could* get better, rather than go back to my comfort zone, a place where it could never get better, at least not to the extent I was looking for. I did not like having to do these things, but I liked doing them more than remaining broke for the rest of my life. I had stepped into the current, and I wasn't going to step out.

CHAPTER 2
INCREASING YOUR INCOME

If you are not one of those fortunate people who already know what you would like to do in business, you are in the majority, and building your own successful business is no less likely because of it.

While waiting in my doctor's office recently, I read an article in one of the news magazines put out for patients to peruse. The article referenced a United States Department of Labor prediction that the generation being schooled right now would hold twelve to fifteen jobs over the course of their lives.

According to the writer, at the time of that article's publication, one-fourth of the working population in the United States had been in their present jobs for less than a year and one-half for less than five.

Anyone who takes a moment to reflect on the implications of that information, if accurate, cannot help but be concerned. The employment realities anticipated for the new generation of workers are layoffs, buyouts, mergers, outsourcings, and the movement of businesses to countries that compete to attract jobs for their workforce populations with lower levels of government regulation and taxes.

Labor is a commodity, just like coal or corn, and, when there is an abundance of it—as there is when a couple of billion residents of developing nations start seeking employment—the working population in any developed country is going to be squeezed by less costly and less regulated global workforces coming available.

The midlife loss of employment or need for a wholesale change of career is about as discouraging as it gets. The most effective way to prepare for such an event is to do so years *before* it becomes necessary—in fact, to prepare for it whether the eventual need to do so appears likely or not. Desperate emergency measures will not suffice. And even if you are in a secure job, the dream of working for yourself is a common desire. This book will help anyone who starts or is running a moneymaking enterprise.

It is my suggestion that it would be wise for you to consider creating at least one source of income that you control. That could be offering a personal service to the marketplace or starting your own business. Either of these could be done part-time.

Where to Start

As a policeman, it didn't take long for me to realize that I was never going to earn enough in law enforcement to provide the life I wanted for my family. After several years of working long hours in a high-risk profession—and holding two jobs on the side—I began to realize I would have to make a change. So, I made a decision to find a way to work for myself.

I tried a few things that just never worked out, and it was quite a few years before I found something to do at which I could make money. I suspect most ambitious men and women have a few failures and false starts, so do not become overly discouraged if the first few things you try don't work.

What *is* important is that you make a firm decision that you will not quit until you have an income, even a part-time one, which you control. You might start with a goal to build an income that is sufficient to provide for your housing expenses, should that ever become necessary.

You might think, "That goal is too small. I want to be rich!" But I think it's a great goal to set. For me, with any objective, it has always worked best to think in terms of the next logical step. That way the goal is not overwhelming. Acorns can grow into oak trees, but it takes time.

If $1,600 a month will keep you in your home, then a goal to earn an extra $400 a week working for yourself is not so large that it freezes out creative thinking. If you find a way to earn an extra $1,600 a month, you could be on the right track to building that into something that can pay you much more.

Many of us would like to work for ourselves, but "doing what?" is always the question. Although most men and women who succeed in business have a particular interest they want to pursue, that is not a requirement—I am proof of that.

For more years than I care to remember, I actually had little enthusiasm for the business I ended up making a comfortable living in. All I knew when I began was that it had the potential to produce more income than driving a police car, and at the time, that was all that mattered to me. Plus, it was the only thing I knew of to try.

So, if you are not one of those fortunate people who already know what you would like to do in business, you are in the majority, and building your own successful business is not less likely because of it.

Sometimes all that is required is just to step into a current where progress is at least possible, whether everything suits you or not. Just getting into a place where a current is flowing in the general direction you want to go is enough for a start.

INCREASING YOUR INCOME

You certainly do not have to have all the answers, and, if you are starting part-time, you don't have to figure out how to earn your entire income from it. Just find something that has the potential to move you forward.

I have a dear friend who has a full-time factory job but works on the side helping property owners with whatever needs to be done. He is bright and efficient and makes almost as much in his spare hours as he makes at his regular job. He has to turn away new accounts. If his factory were to shut down, he would have a relatively smooth transition to his next job, or to full-time self-employment. His work may seem trivial to someone wanting to build a big business, but that is not my point. He is using his skills, enjoys his side business, sets his own work schedule, and, over the course of a few years has secured his family's needs no matter what happens at his factory job.

As in everything, if your life-path gives you some sort of head start, such as a parent who has succeeded in a particular business, do not be too quick to dismiss the advantage. Your odds can be greatly increased anywhere you have someone willing to help. There is no better education than hands-on in the real world, particularly if you also have a willing mentor.

There is no academic education that can replace what four to six years of hands-on experience can teach you. And, if you choose to attend college, avoid foolish levels of debt to finance it. Technical schools are affordable and a better choice for many. **A man or woman with an in-demand skill clearly has a path to business ownership.**

And on occasion, an inspired idea for a business will just come in the course of daily life. I have heard of this often. But, and this is important, you should be encouraging that possibility by thinking about being in business for yourself. "Doing what" is not the question. It is cultivating a passionate interest that can lead to the inspired idea.

THE ENTRY-LEVEL CEO

As many of you are in business for yourselves, either now or will be in the future, I will turn our conversation now specifically to how to build and run a business in such a way that the odds of success are greatly increased—how, in other words, to become an entry-level CEO.

Building a Business

Despite serious reservations about the wisdom of the move, when I was twenty-eight years old, I left the police department I worked for and went to work with my stepfather in his modest roofing business. I was less than enthusiastic about being involved in that line of work, and that is putting it mildly.

But I also knew that few people, if any, have everything come to them just the way they want it, and there was one thing I was certain about: if I did not try to do something about my future when a reasonable opportunity was presented, then I was probably already living about as well as I ever would.

Few people get to choose that which suits them best from a host of options. Opportunities are rarely made to order. They usually have to be seized and improved upon.

I decided I would work with my stepfather for a short time and then move on to something more suitable to me. Well, nothing better ever came along, and to my credit, no matter how much I didn't like what I was doing, I refused to quit. Of all the costly things a man may do, quitting one job just because he doesn't like it before he has another job to go to is near the top of the list.

My stepfather, Frank, was an impulsive entrepreneur, which I think is better than always holding back. But the unvarnished truth is that he was no businessman when it came to putting system to his efforts. And, because Frank was typical of most men and women who start a business of their own, his company could not grow because he didn't understand how to build an organized business.

As a result, I was handed a constant stream of problems to solve, in addition to the overall conundrum of trying to make the business profitable. Of course, I couldn't see any benefit to it at the time, but this training was invaluable to my future and I learned a lot from it: mostly what not to do.

Despite the tension caused by our different views toward business, my stepfather and I had a sincere mutual respect for each other's strengths, and he had many, and we deferred to one another whenever one felt strongly about an issue. We worked together for more than ten years before Frank retired, and it was my privilege to see to it that the business supported him and my mother up to the time he passed away.

I still take care of my mother and make sure she is provided for financially, which is something I never could have done as a police officer. I mention this because the ability to help loved ones in meaningful ways financially is one of the great downstream benefits of going into business.

Today, that business—Echols Roofing & Home Improvements, in Atlanta, Georgia—on occasion does as much as $100,000 in business in a single day when the economy is strong, and talented men and women produce that revenue without much help from me. As I am going to offer advice about building a business, I will set proper modesty aside for a moment to share with you a few facts about my own.

For twenty-two consecutive years, at the time of this writing, Echols Roofing & Home Improvements has been listed as a "Best Pick of the Industry" by leading Atlanta area consumer report guides on contractors. For the thirty-plus years I have been in charge, we have never been the object of a lawsuit, never had to sue a customer for any reason, never had a single customer refuse to pay us (that I can recall), and have never been late in paying a single bill.

These facts would be amazing enough for any business, but I think even more so for a company that works on people's most cherished possession—their homes. Additionally,

I have had only one employee ever sustain a lost-time injury and have filed only one claim against my general liability policy for damage to a customer's residence. And that claim, which happened about thirty years ago, was just $1,500, for a soiled rug.

An employee of one of the largest material suppliers to my industry told me that among the vendors that supply Atlanta contractors, who because of their position know how well each of the companies are operated, my company is considered one of the "gold standard" accounts. Assuming his perception is anywhere near correct, it is quite an informed compliment.

It takes a lot more than wanting to earn more money to build a great reputation in business. The entry-level CEO will need the ability to put the right people in the right job and model a strong sense of responsibility to customers, employees, and creditors to earn that opinion. Whether it is completely deserved or not, I am careful to protect that perception of my company in everything we do.

For whatever benefit you may derive from it, I will now share with you a few things I learned from building my own business that I think would be helpful to anyone who decides to start a business of his or her own.

What Determines Success?

Many attributes may contribute to success, such as suitability to the work, persistence, and a pleasing personality, but these things do not *determine* success because many people have succeeded without them.

Years ago, I read a book from the early part of the last century that talked about success in a way that has stuck with me. In 1927 Brown Landone wrote *The Success Process*. In it, he stated that success is determined by only four things:

INCREASING YOUR INCOME

1. The willingness to act on your own ideas.
2. A decision not to be stopped by any particular thing that hinders you. (This, I would point out, would include a lack of specialized knowledge because you do not have to possess that knowledge personally. Specialized knowledge is one of the most easily purchased commodities on earth.)
3. Rendering service in sufficient quantity.
4. Requiring that you receive fair compensation for the service you render.

Many other things may be helpful, but only what you do about these four actually *determine* whether or not you will succeed.

When you are managing a business, always ask yourself, "Which of these four determinants is my weak point right now? Which is the most immediately needful for me to address? What would be a logical step to start making progress with that issue?" Keep doing that and you will see progress, for only what you do about these four will determine the results from your efforts.

*Success in business is the result
of a constant series of small actions
directed toward improving
these four determinants.*

I believe there are two additional ingredients to add to the process in order to build a business that is not only successful but will also give you a *satisfactory lifestyle*:

1. Do not stop at working for yourself. Make owning a business that can take care of you your goal.

2. With talented others build a business that systematically and fluidly delivers a consistently superior product or service to the customer without requiring your daily direct involvement to accomplish the sales or the service.

Combining these six "determinants of success" will allow you to own a business that is successful and profitable *and* have a lifestyle that does not drive you to exhaustion.

The rest of this book will focus on how to attain these outcomes.

The Number One Mistake

Question: What is the number one mistake I see small business owners make?

Answer: Hands down, the biggest and most common mistake I see is starting a business with no understanding of what a successful business should look like.

Too many would-be entry-level CEOs confuse working for themselves with owning a business. Therefore, they grind for an entire lifetime but never build a business that can take care of them. When you own a business, you have the option of limiting your involvement to general oversight while more capable men and women actually deliver the goods or services.

*If you are a one-man show
or if your business cannot function without you, then, unless
your business can be sold
for a large amount of money,
you do not own a business yet.
You are still building one.*

INCREASING YOUR INCOME

Now, one caveat: nothing said here is meant to apply to professional men and women who are themselves, because of their skills and education, their own "business". Their specialized knowledge is the real asset of their chosen business. Even so, something in this book may spark a thought that could be helpful to you lawyers, doctors, CPA's, financial planners and professionals of every sort to improve your position.

By my definition, *business ownership* is a system of human activity that can profitably deliver quality products or services in a fluid manner without direct every-day involvement from the owner.

If you work for yourself and your income would stop if you did not go to work, then, to my way of thinking, you do not yet own a business. You may very well be building a business, but until it can produce very close to the same income without you, you just own your own job. If you must be personally involved for the business to operate, your income can be stopped tomorrow by one accident. Is that "owning a business"?

This is not to say that no involvement from you is ever required. The old saying attributed to Benjamin Franklin—

He that by the plough would thrive
Himself must either hold or drive.

—is always true. In business, as in everything else in life, if you take your hand away from the steering wheel long enough, there is going to be a wreck. Anyone who thinks he or she can walk away from his or her affairs, no matter what those affairs are, and leave all oversight of the business and money to others, will sooner or later become very busy trying to recover from that error.

Make this your objective from the start:

Create an organization that delivers products or services in a fluid manner and with the highest standards of ethics and quality *without your direct involvement in the sale or service.* I spend two to three hours a day coordinating what my team does, I do it from a home on my farm, and I enjoy it. The used key is brightest.

In the beginning, a young entrepreneur will be doing everything himself or herself. As soon as possible, he or she will usually hire administrative help to free up time so they can keep bringing in business. Unfortunately, that is as far as many get in delegating their business affairs to others.

Here's what I suggest: replace yourself in sales as soon as you can and then replace yourself in mid-level management; or as is the case with my business, in direct field oversight of the jobs.

If you wish to own a business that can take care of you, it is imperative that you build a system of human activity that smoothly delivers what you supply to the marketplace.

Of course, you will have to determine how to fairly compensate these people while keeping fixed overhead costs as low as possible. Salaried personnel may have to be responsible for more than one job, and in some positions, it may be best to have compensation tied directly to production rather than fixed salaries.

This process varies from one business to the next. The goal is to minimize the amount of money you have to produce each week just to pay the bills.

One more time before we move on to more specific guidelines:

> *When you own a business,*
> *your absence should not affect your income*
> *or the product quality.*

Only by delegating your responsibilities to other proficient and dependable men and women who are good at what they do and enjoy it, is your business income secured.

INCREASING YOUR INCOME

Other than brief periods when business is exceptionally brisk or challenging, your direct involvement in routine daily business matters should not be a requirement.

My highest income weeks have all occurred during periods when I was away from the business. (And I hope that is just a coincidence!)

Granted, it may take years of work to get there, but building a business that can provide your income without you working early to late every day should be in the center of your planning and hiring from the beginning.

A business owner should be working toward a reasonably smooth process and a fairly steady income—whether he or she is on vacation for a few weeks or away building another income-producing enterprise. Anyone who owns a business needs to be attentive to that business, but others should be performing the day-to-day functions.

I am at my business almost every day. But two to three hours in the morning is sufficient to keep me fully aware and in control of operations. The business would do close to as well if I had to be absent for a while.

You don't have to be doing twenty million a year to make this happen. My business makes enough money for me to live comfortably and there are only about eight key positions I rely on to keep the jobs running smoothly and the customers happy.

Notwithstanding my own fortunate experience, I wish to state clearly:

I do not know of any guaranteed formula for succeeding in business,
and I don't believe one exists.

There are just too many variables in the natures of various businesses and the strengths and weaknesses of the men and women running them. We all just have to take our shot and adjust as we go.

THE ENTRY-LEVEL CEO

What can help any of us—and help us a lot—is counsel from someone ahead of us in the process, particularly written advice which can be re-read often to keep us on track in our "big-picture" thinking.

There are no guarantees for any of us when we begin. In the next chapter, I will explain what I did differently from the vast majority of ambitious men and women who start a business of their own and then slowly drown in it.

To be open and honest, I did not plan much of what ended up helping me, and I tend to forget all the things I tried that didn't work. But I found my way to a good place, and now, in hindsight, can identify a few things I did right that turned out to be really important.

Not every point will be applicable to you, but a conversation with any debt-free and contented business owner should be helpful to someone seeking to become an entry-level CEO.

CHAPTER 3
TEN BUSINESS GUIDELINES

We set the customers' expectations and the standards by which we shall be judged with the very words that come out of our own mouths.

Remember: your goal should be to build a business that supports you and allows for a satisfactory lifestyle. That means creating an organization that delivers products or services in a fluid manner, with the highest standards of ethics and quality, without your direct involvement in the sale or service.

Allow me to share with you the ten guidelines that made it possible for me—and can help you do the same.

Here are my rules for running my business:

1. Hire the best available.

2. Train thoroughly in every detail; explain the "why" for every rule.

3. Monitor employee performance. Correct right away, praise right away.

4. Establish rules that protect fluidity and allow no exceptions to those rules.
5. Teach everyone to run toward problems, not away from them.
6. As far as possible, make everything about doing business with your company a "Disney quality" experience.
7. Avoid problematic customers and learn which projects to avoid.
8. Do not take work without enough profit to justify the effort.
9. Keep a financial margin for safety in your business accounts.
10. Apply the Golden Rule in every instance with employees and customers.

1. Hire The Best

As your business grows, the object is to replace yourself at each position with men and women who are better at it than you are. Look for someone who "wows" you with his or her work skills and diligence during a six-month trial period.

My mother once told me, "Mark, you can't know what is really inside another person until you have lived or worked with them for six months." The way I apply that wisdom is to always hire with the spoken understanding: "Let's try it for six months, and if either of us feels it is not a good fit, we will part as friends."

If I see an employee who does not have what I am looking for, I will release them. Personally, I would prefer to be understaffed and have to pass on some work then keep a less-than-satisfactory employee on the payroll and have the stress of dealing with the mess later. You may make a little more money if you keep someone just because you are busy, but it's at the risk of a lot more trouble.

However, I also suggest you place a very high value on loyalty. If you find someone that puts the customer and the company first and is making an effort to fit in and improve, then find a way to make it work. I have had to be patient with some of my best income producers for close to a year, but they had the character I was looking for. Skills can be learned. Character is set. You don't make cream; you find it.

If you keep someone on because they are good at their job, but they lack character, my experience is that you will eventually pay dearly for it. If you have someone who is not going to work out, but, for a time, you absolutely must keep him or her on, quietly get busy finding a replacement, and don't keep putting it off.

If you can't find a suitable employee for a position you need filled, you will have to keep turning people over until you find the right one. I have talked to high-level managers in some of the largest companies in America, and, big or small, we all do it the same way: be willing to make changes until you have found what you were looking for.

Here are a few of the more subtle things I consider when hiring, though these are by no means foolproof:

Did they quit their last job before they had a better one to go to?

Rashness is a bad sign. It indicates a hot temper, poor judgment, or immaturity.

How many people are they responsible for supporting at home? How much money do they owe and for what? Is it well within expectations that, with you, they will earn an income sufficient to meet their needs?

I once had an applicant who needed $80,000 a year to meet his obligations. He could make that with me during very good years, but not in tight ones. Why hire someone you know in advance cannot earn what they will need while working for you? Don't let a new hire's money problems become *your* employee problem.

Have they been divorced several times?

Once is the majority these days. Three times is a red flag that there is disorder somewhere.

Find some pretense to walk them out to their car and look it over. Discreetly drive by their home.

Is the car clean, inside and out? Are the yard and home exterior well kept? Anyone with an orderly mind will not tolerate uncleanliness and disorder around him or her. This is one rule that is universally reliable.

I don't care about the price range of these things. I am looking at the *conditions* this man or woman is comfortable living in. They will be bringing exactly that into your business.

Do they use their religious faith to suggest they are a better hire for you?

That is a reliable indicator of trouble. I am not suggesting that some legitimate remark such as, "I will need Sundays off for services" is a problem. I am looking for something more overt.

I once had an applicant tell me, "I'm a Christian. I hope you don't mind that." There was no reason for that comment at that point in our conversation. For me, he was no longer under consideration because this was simply a clumsy attempt at manipulation.

TEN BUSINESS GUIDELINES

As soon as you get someone like that—using religious faith to manipulate your opinion or jockey for favor—know for a certainty you are looking at your next headache if you hire! When you hire you are looking for skilled men and women of character with good sense and a work ethic. These qualities are found in people of every faith, and in those of no particular religious inclination at all.

2. Train Thoroughly

You owe it to your employees to train them well in every detail and to explain the "why" for every rule. People follow rules more willingly when they understand the reason for them.

If you are hiring people to work efficiently without your constant supervision, they need to understand exactly what you want them to do, what the best practices are for their jobs, and why you have certain requirements. Then provide daily feedback with corrections and approval once they begin.

For reference, here are some of the crucial things I teach each associate—and require them to observe.

Never fail to perform anything exactly as and when you said (or even implied) you would.

When I discuss this requirement with new hires, they readily agree to the rule. In fact, according to the perception they have of themselves, they already work this way. The truth is, however, with extremely rare exceptions, they do not and never have performed to standards this exacting, but they don't realize it.

Nearly all employees must learn from experience what this rule means—and that it is meant literally. I do not even allow an employee not to keep a commitment they only *implied*. And, during the first six months with a new employee, it is usually necessary to have several conversations to explain exactly what it means not even to imply a commitment unless they are sure they can keep it.

For example, an employee may tell a customer, "I'll try to be there Thursday afternoon if I can get finished with the other job I am on in time to come." If the business of the day prevents them from showing up, they may not think they have broken any trust, and since they did not set a firm appointment, they may not even feel the need to call the customer.

But in a well-run business, every commitment—even an *implied* one—is honored. Of course, this means company representatives must learn to be very careful about what they say.

As an example: Explaining to a new hire what a proper response is to a potential customer asking when they can expect an appointment when that answer cannot be given with certainty, might go like this:

"If the day's business allows it, I may be able to come Thursday afternoon. But, as I will not know for sure until Thursday afternoon, you should not change your plans, as I am only guessing. If I can come that day, I will call you as soon as I know, to see if it is convenient for you. If I can't come, I'll call as soon as I know that as well. That is as much of an honest answer as I can give you now. Your request for service is important to all of us here, and as soon as I can, I will arrange to be there. And once I start working for you, I will give you the same courtesy. I won't be neglecting my work for you to make appointments elsewhere. At Echols Home Improvements we are not even allowed to imply commitments and then not keep them. I am sure you can appreciate that. I hope that is the kind of company you want, even if you have to wait for an appointment."

What is there for a customer to complain about then? Though the meet-up with the customer may happen on that day, the promise is for a phone call, not a meeting. The employee then sets a reminder to make that phone call on their smart phone.

This exacting standard of conduct is so unusual, it will rarely happen unless the business leader requires it. Most

TEN BUSINESS GUIDELINES

men or women that are scrupulous about watching and honoring their words and commitments are already owners, not employees. And several decades of experience have proven that, unless there is a dire emergency, customers willingly cooperate with that type of truthful, respectful interaction. *We set the customers' expectations and the standards by which we shall be judged with the very words that come out of our own mouths.*

I live in a rural area. I once called for a plumber, and after I told him to go ahead with the work, he said he would be back in a few days. I was busy, so I left it to him and returned to my business.

A few weeks later, it occurred to me the work had not been done. When I called and asked him where in the heck he had been, he actually said, "I am only two weeks late." As a business owner, what you accept, you teach.

Now, some customers will attempt to force a commitment for more than can be promised. In such a case, your employee must understand they are to stand their ground as politely and firmly as needed, rather than be bullied into some commitment they may not be able to meet.

I recently had a customer call and ask for the owner. She had signed a contract to make home improvements, but as the weather had been rainy, the job start had been delayed. The weeks forecast called for no clearing. She told me how long she'd been waiting and demanded I give her a start date. I explained the risks to her property due to weather and why a commitment could not be made until the forecast cleared. She said that was unsatisfactory because she had to make plans.

I told her, "Anyone of good faith would accept that I cannot make a commitment to start with a weather forecast that calls for uninterrupted rain. You will have to wait, just as we will." She said that was an unacceptable response. I told her, "But that *is* your answer. I think you should take your business somewhere else."

I will not be forced into making a promise I cannot keep, nor will I work for an imperious or irrational customer—and I make that the firm policy for everyone that works for me. They appreciate that. And, by the way, "Mrs. Smith, I am sorry if you are disappointed, but that *is* the only truthful answer I can give," politely but firmly stated, is a good line to remember when dealing with a pushy person.

Under-promise and Over-deliver

This closely follows the previous rule. *We* set the expectations of our customers. The words spoken by your own representatives are what your company will be judged by. For that reason, they should always promise a little less than they can actually deliver. That way, they have room for exceeding expectations.

In my business of home improvements, we are often asked, "How much will we be inconvenienced? What will it be like while the job is going on?" We tell them, "This is loud, noisy, dirty, difficult, dangerous, and very inconvenient work. When we finish it will be clean, and we will certainly straighten up at the end of each day. But there is no way to have a crew of men working on your home without inconvenience to you."

> Employees who feel well paid and appreciated and customers who feel special is the goal.

What can they get upset with after that explanation? We have set the expectations and left room to provide a much more pleasant experience than is anticipated. We have under-promised—so we can over-deliver.

If a customer asks how long a job will take, and we expect a four-day project, we will tell the customer it could take five days—and then try to surprise them by exceeding the expectations we have set. That way, even if something unanticipated slows the job down, we still have a day to deal with it and remain on schedule.

But what do most people in business do? They tell the customer whatever they think the customer wants to hear in order to get the contract.

You can apply this to any business you are in. You set the expectations; therefore, set expectations you can meet or exceed. The difference in customer satisfaction very often is not the quality of work, but a comparison in their own minds between what they expected and what they experienced. Two jobs can be done in the same time frame with the same level of proficiency, and one customer can be complaining and the other happy.

The final impression customers have from doing business with you is largely a result of the expectations you or your representative gave them before any of the work even began.

Resolving complaints comes before new business

The owner of a business must let all employees—indeed, everyone connected with the organization—know from the start that customer service is a higher priority than new business.

This does not mean customer service calls can always be handled as soon as the customer would prefer, as they may come during a particularly difficult time, but those calls are always handled as expeditiously as circumstances allow. Customer service calls are higher priorities than calls from potential customers who have not yet given you their business.

When a customer complaint comes into my office, it is dispatched immediately, and once a week I personally review any requests for customer service to see to it they were not relegated by a busy employee to when-I-can-get-to-it status.

In a properly run business, monies are set aside to cover service after the sale, which should allow for all legitimate complaints to be resolved quickly and in a first-class manner.

Try to handle complaints in a way that will turn an unhappy customer into a fan and a vocal promoter of your firm.

Happy employees and customers are every executive's goal. My dear friend and mentor, the late Ed Sayad—one of the top executives who built the UPS company into what it is today—once told me, "Mark, unless you are dealing with microbes in a lab, all that any thriving business is, is *happy people!*" Employees who feel well paid and appreciated and customers who feel special is the goal.

When you train your employees thoroughly and make sure they understand the "why" of every rule, when you give heartfelt praise for extra effort or work well done, and considerately given suggestions for improvement, when you look for and acknowledge good judgment and good work, you can build an effective workforce. That is what results in satisfied customers.

3. Monitor Employee Performance

Earlier in this chapter, we pointed out that only by delegating responsibilities to other dependable, skilled men and women can your income from your business be made reasonably reliable.

However, delegation has two parts: the assignment *and* the follow-up to verify how well the assignment was performed. When you are too busy to check up on the quality of the work being done, you have handed your employees your wallet. Not a good idea.

This is another bit of wisdom from my mother: "No matter how much you think of someone, never turn control of your business or your money over to somebody else."

This oversight does not have to come from you personally. In my business, I have skilled supervisors who monitor the work in order to prevent poor performance from occurring. I am notified in a timely manner if there is a recurring problem.

TEN BUSINESS GUIDELINES

Until you have reliable people in that position, follow this trustworthy advice: do not accept an employee's explanations at face value. Until your business is too large to make it practical, look well into every customer complaint personally. You will learn much from this about your personnel that you can learn in no other way.

The other critical aspect of monitoring employees is following up on both good and bad performance. My advice is to *correct right away and praise right away.*

Reinforce good performance and smart decisions by telling the employee what they did well and that it is appreciated. On the other hand, overlooked problems do not correct themselves; they only get worse over time. It is best to confront mistakes and make corrections immediately. This lets the employee know that *you know* what is being done.

Whatever you accept, you teach.

It is important that you do not accept excuses. If you will accept excuses from employees—or you don't know your business or your employee well enough to know the difference between an excuse and a genuine problem—you are going to get more excuses and more problems. People need and perform best with empathetic, but accountable, supervision.

Here is an interesting story I read years ago. An elementary school had a small, fenced playground. They decided to remove the fence to give the children more room to play. However, instead of using the liberty, the children stayed close to each other and remained even nearer the center of the playground. The fence evidently made them feel secure. Businesses and homes with firm protective boundaries bring out the best in us because humans need boundaries.

Within my own business, I know the difference between an explanation of facts and an excuse, however plausibly presented. When I am hearing an excuse, I tell the person

I am talking to, "If I want to hear stories, I can turn on the television. Here is what you should have done and what I want you to do now."

Here's an example from my business just last week. A customer signed a contract and selected material colors, among other things. The materials were ordered, but afterward, the customer changed his mind and altered one color choice. A second order was prepared, correcting the first and sent to the supplier. But the supplier shipped the original color, which was now wrong.

I asked my employee what had happened. I was told we had done our part in notifying the supplier of the change, but that someone over there had dropped the ball.

Well, anyone who will accept that rationale will only get more of it. In a tone no one could mistake for agreement, I let my employee know the mistake was still totally his responsibility and explained why:

> *If we sent that order to begin with, then it was our responsibility alone to see to it that the order was corrected with no room for error.*
>
> *What you did was obviously insufficient as the mix-up still occurred. You sent a corrected order. But where was the first order? Someone still had it over there.*
>
> *You should have called and said, "Pull up that order on the computer while I wait. Now delete it. Are there any hard copies? Is there now any possibility that someone in shipping has our original, and now incorrect order, anywhere in the system? No? Okay, good. That order has been changed by the customer and will be turned away if you ship it. I am now sending you the corrected order."*

Everyone likes working in an orderly business where they know everyone else is doing their job well, even when they

TEN BUSINESS GUIDELINES

are the ones getting a reasonably administered correction. Don't accept excuses. But it is even worse to accuse someone of making an excuse when what they really need is your help.

Remember, as the boss, it is your responsibility to delegate, and also to monitor the performance of your team at key points so that the business runs as smoothly as possible. Avoiding frustrations adds greatly to the satisfaction of all employees, and to the success of your business.

Also, however, remember that delegating responsibilities to others does not mean you give up control. Businesses must always be guided with strong and responsible hands. Never turn the financial controls of your business affairs over to someone else. When it comes to the money maintain prudential oversight.

> You must take good care of whatever takes care of you.

You must take good care of whatever takes care of you.

4. Establish Rules That Protect Fluidity

Do not tolerate sand in the machine. There can be no exception to the rules that keep your business machine running smoothly. Maintaining an orderly, pleasant, and profitable work atmosphere is everyone's job.

Again, what you accept you teach. I am such a stickler for avoiding friction that my salespeople know, if they sell a job to a petulant and arrogant customer or sell a project so problematic it will cause great difficulty for the workmen, they risk their own pay for it.

Most of the headaches so common to owners of businesses can and should be avoided simply by avoiding the wrong people and the wrong projects. I tell my employees, "The money you might make from selling the wrong job, if you ever actually get paid, is never worth it."

An alert owner should be sensitive to friction anywhere. If you can't run an organized business your customers won't be happy, and your employees won't be either. Problems get bigger the longer they are tolerated. Be observant for anything—or anyone—that causes chafing. Whatever wears down employees or frustrates rational customers should be avoided.

5. Teach Everyone To Run Toward Problems

It is human nature to wish to avoid unpleasant situations and angry customers. However, running away from problems is the worst reaction from a business standpoint.

In fact, every disappointment is an opportunity to prove to a customer how wise they were to give your company their business. If I have a situation in which my company has disappointed a rational customer, I try to make that customer so pleased with the way the problem is addressed that they become a walking advertisement for my company.

Even though I personally am not involved in daily problem-solving at my business, every employee knows my policy: "If there is any doubt about what we are responsible to do, then do what you would do if it were your own home and I will pay you for it."

Of course, this guideline applies to us CEOs, too. No running away. If you are the boss, be the boss, and take the really tough problems on yourself.

I have many employees so capable at what they do that, even when tough problems arise, they often handle everything from beginning to end and tell me later what happened and what they did about it. If necessary, however, the problem comes to me.

TEN BUSINESS GUIDELINES

6. Make Everything "Disney Quality"

Years ago, my wife and I took our children to Disney World. When we arrived, one of my daughters became quite ill. As we were checking in, I asked a Disney employee how to get to the nearest medical facility, explaining that I had a sick child. They didn't give me directions. Instead, five minutes later they had a Disney employee drive us in a courtesy vehicle to the local medical center.

Saying that I was impressed is an understatement. I learned a lot from that level of service, and today I try to give my customers a "Disney quality" experience.

This begins with a commitment to good communications with all customers. The objective is to keep the customer so fully informed that he or she feels "in the loop" at all times.

If customers are regularly calling with questions, especially if they are the same questions over and over, you have a process to correct. Every time a customer calls to ask for clarification about something, you might want to ask yourself, "Could that call from the customer have been avoided had we done something differently?" If it could have been avoided, then make the procedural change necessary to keep it from happening with future customers. And in keeping with our rule never to over-promise, don't make a commitment just to appease a customer unless you know you can keep it.

Communication with customers is just the beginning. Let me illustrate with an example of a recent incident that resulted in a "wow!" response from one of my customers. A gentleman had contracted with my firm to do some work at his home. On the first day of the job, as he was backing his car out of the driveway, he backed into our dumpster at the jobsite, damaging the car's bumper.

He called to complain, though he had been told a dumpster would be delivered to his drive that morning, and, of course, he alone was responsible for looking where he was going when driving his car. I tactfully made that point to him but then said, "However, to show you that your confidence in my company is well placed, get an estimate to repair the car and send it to me. I'll mail you a check."

I could relate many such incidents. This level of customer complaint resolution is the norm in my company. Is it any wonder I do not have to rely on an expensive advertising budget? My customers are my walking, talking advertisements. Delivering "Disney quality" service will cost money occasionally, but you will make it back many times over.

A woman called me last week with a particularly difficult construction problem, one we could not help her with because I scrupulously avoid such situations. In similar instances, most companies would just tell her, "I'm sorry, but that's not something we do." But I knew that, on her own, she would have almost no chance of locating the right person qualified to help her.

So, although I was quite busy that day, I gave her fifteen minutes on the phone to offer some guidance and then asked that she let me make some calls on her behalf. Two days later, I had arranged an appointment for her with the right company to solve her problem. I did this without expecting anything in return. She had come to me for help, and I went the extra mile.

The last thing she said to me was, "I don't know how to thank you. What you did is so unusual. I told my husband about it, too. We both agreed, when we need future home improvements we will call only your company."

Just today, an employee informed me that a manufacturer had kept one of his customers waiting two months for a door to be made and delivered. Then, when it finally arrived, it was damaged. The supplier and the manufacturer advised him of another lengthy delay to replace it. The customer was angry, and I didn't blame him one bit, I would have been, too.

I asked for the customer's number and called him. Most contractors would just explain what the client already knows: we can't control manufacturers or shippers. But that's a waste of everyone's time because what the customer really wants is his job finished, and I cannot do that in a timely manner for reasons totally beyond my control.

So, I told him, truthfully, that even though this manufacturer was nationally known and the product often requested, any future customer who chooses that manufacturer would be warned of the risk of poor service ahead of time. I also told him I would get on the phone with that company and "put a stone in their shoe" and then follow up with him on the results of that call. Further, I reduced his bill by ten percent for the inconvenience, even though the problem was not my fault.

He went from being angry with us to being my enthusiastic ally in the problem. That is the "Disney quality" result you want.

By the way, the employee who notified me of this customer's problem told me he had spent many hours trying to solve it before bringing it to me. I told him I appreciated his extra effort and was paying him a bonus on the job for going the extra mile. The job will now be a breakeven for me, but a boon for that employee's appreciative commitment to me in the future—and for that customer's positive word of mouth recommendations, which is the best advertising in the world.

I was on the phone last week with a former employee who had spent his life in the home-improvement trades. His last job had been a few years spent working for me. He is in failing health now, due to a debilitating disease. In a raspy but cheerful voice he called to chat and, during the conversation, said, "Boss, before I pass on I want you to know that you were the best employer I ever worked for." I replied, "That may be the most meaningful praise I have ever received here. Thank you, Clark."

Building a business that provides "Disney quality" experiences to customers requires authority, but an authority exercised in and tempered by respect for what each employee is doing for you. Striking this balance well and consistently is the goal of the effective business owner/manager.

Here is one more suggestion for all entry-level CEO's. Keep a small personal recorder in your pocket at all times. Every time you make a commitment to someone to do something, think of a task you need to complete, or have any thought you want to capture, put it on the recorder. That way, nothing slips through the cracks in the press of the days many business details or is forgotten. Each morning I "clear" my recorder by listening to each entry and then performing each task.

That is the best way I know of to be an effective owner that does not lose track of the many "moving parts" of daily business. A "Disney" quality company comes from a CEO that does not lose track of details. That means you must have a system for performing your daily business that does not rely solely on memory.

7. Avoid Problematic Customers

Avoid strident or imperious customers and any deeply problematic jobs. Do not involve the company in any arrangement that will exhaust and frustrate your workforce. Every business has jobs that should be avoided. *You want your competitors to have those jobs.*

After a few violations of this rule, you will certainly learn how to apply it for yourself. I teach this guideline: if there are three tough difficulties within one job, I pass on it. In other words, three strikes and you're out. Of course, one really big one is sometimes enough, too.

No matter what type of business you go into, there will be some jobs and some customers you just need to avoid. It is in your emotional and financial interest to develop a way to identify them before business is entered into. Exactly what to avoid varies with the type of business you are in and perhaps can only be learned the hard way from a few mistakes. Just make sure you learn what not to do from these events.

8. Do Not Take Work Without Enough Profit

This guideline is so important, it warrants a chapter of its own—the next chapter, "The 80/20 Rule." Successful businesses require fair compensation. Period.

9. Keep A Financial Safety Margin

Providing a "Disney quality" experience to our customers sometimes requires extra expense. How do I provide for that? Very simply.

Each month I set aside money, whatever I can afford that month, in a separate company savings account until the total equals an amount I know is sufficient to take care of any customer service issues. Then I keep adding to this account until I also have a buffer against unexpected large events.

That account is always available, though rarely used, and allows me the mental comfort of knowing I can reach behind me and cover unexpected bills or even a payroll if I need to.

A responsible business owner should have money set aside in a separate account for use in event of unanticipated need. If you have been in business for years and do not have an account set up to serve as an emergency fund or to service customers, you are missing a simple step to make your business, and your life, more comfortable and secure.

I also keep enough extra cash in the business checking account to buffer the ups and downs of daily cash flow. The appropriate amount will vary from business to business, but every company has, on occasion, both unexpectedly large bills and slow receivables. Until your business can cover those two events simultaneously, your company is not sufficiently funded.

Books which teach accounting principles will explain that so much idle cash is not the best use of funds and that any excess operating capital should be directed where it can make profits for shareholders. That may be true with large companies, but speaking for myself, with smaller companies I think my policy is best. A well-run business, no matter what size—but especially a smaller business—has a duty to become independent in regard to routine daily cash flow issues as soon as possible.

But what do most small business owners do? They take every dime they can out of the company to support their lifestyle—and then have to scramble when things get tight.

Remember this: if you run a business, that business, along with its suppliers and customers, *comes before **you***—period! That is caring for the goose that lays the eggs and keeps the eggs coming.

My wife, Tracy, explained it this way and although I referenced it a little earlier in this book it is worth repeating: "You have to take good care of whatever takes care of you!"

There may be many years early on when there just isn't enough money, but if your business ever turns the corner, don't start lighting your cigars with hundred dollar bills right away. Instead, make your business bulletproof.

I was watching an interview on the Bloomberg channel with a successful businessman named John Koss. His business had been through a bankruptcy, and he had rebuilt it. He was asked by the interviewer, "What did you learn from the experience?" His reply was rich in wisdom. Mr. Koss said, "You don't run a business on borrowed cash. You keep a line of credit, but you don't use it. To do this, fixed expenses must be kept low. The only way expenses can be kept at sustainable levels low enough to accomplish this is if every employee does two or three jobs instead of one."

TEN BUSINESS GUIDELINES

I took care of my business first. Then, as I could take a little money out of it, I first paid off my personal debts. For many years, instead of consuming my earnings, I just took the small but growing amount of money my business was earning and pushed it forward to cover future contingencies. I made the business healthy first, then myself, by following the steps outlined in the first book in this series, *Riches Beyond the Bling*.

I continued doing this until there was nothing left to pay off. This took me twenty years, but those years greatly changed the rest of my life. Of course, as I have explained elsewhere, I did spend some of that money along the way, too.

If this sounds severe to you, what do you think you should be using your productive years for? To create more future obligations? To own more *things*, things which require your money and time for maintenance? No thanks.

Bottom line: a well-run business should not be relying on borrowed money to cover the day-to-day cash needs common to its operation. Keep a financial buffer always at the ready. If you have the judgment not to abuse it, a business line of credit with your local bank would be something to consider as well. If you wait until you urgently need the credit line, it will be too late to qualify for it.

One more important point: do not assume that sales equal profits. I believe eight out of ten small business owners in any line of work make this assumption, and it is foolish to the point of absurdity. Don't be one of them. Profits are what is left after *all* direct and indirect expenses; and profits are what it takes to survive and then, to thrive.

So don't become fixated on competitors who sell at prices that will not allow them to survive long term, much less ever thrive. Business owners rightfully weigh their prices against the marketplace, but the fact is, if you work, you must do that business at a price that actually allows you to keep your business healthy and get fairly paid personally. Fairness to your own family requires it.

10. Apply The Golden Rule

In every circumstance, to the best of your human ability, put yourself into the shoes of your customers and your employees and ask, "If I were in their position, what would I wish to be done?" This goes hand in hand with providing a "Disney quality" experience.

Each year, I have a company conduct phone interviews with approximately three hundred of my previous year's customers and record their comments, which are sent to me. The satisfaction rate runs about 98 percent year after year. The researcher told me this is an unheard-of satisfaction rate, except for the small "one-man" type of business in which a very responsible owner is performing every task. The Golden Rule has a lot to do with our high satisfaction rate.

When I am dealing with a legitimate customer concern or complaint, I never ask myself, "What is my legal obligation here?" I ask myself, "What would be the right thing to do? What would exceed a reasonable customer's expectation in this situation? What response to this customer service issue would cause a 'wow' in me if I were on the other side of this?"

Since I do this as a matter of course and have for years, individual incidents are truthfully hard to recall. It's just another business decision, and then I move on. However, to make sure I am clearly communicating what I mean, I will give you details of a few recent "Golden Rule" decisions I made.

A roof treatment procedure performed by my company did not perform to expectations. The manufacturer could offer no solution to the satisfaction of the customer. Since the customer had relied on our guidance when choosing the product, I gave him his money back—all $10,000 of it—and took the loss myself.

A second example of Golden Rule customer service: I recently received a phone call from a man who thought he was being overcharged. He wanted to talk to me about it before he wrote the check. I looked into it and determined he was not being overcharged but knew that nothing I could say would dissuade him from his opinion.

So, I asked him what he thought would have been a fair price. He told me, and I said, "I have looked at the contract, and you were charged competitive market rates. But your opinion of us is more important than a few dollars. I appreciate your business and I want you to feel free to use us again or refer us. Write the check for the amount you named, and I will accept it as payment in full."

Then I added, in a humorous tone, "But the next time you feel this way, call me *before* we do the work!" It was only a matter of a few hundred dollars. And would you believe he still complained about us and wrote scathing reviews online about us? He did. But that did not bother me at all. It truly didn't. We are promised we will reap what we sow. We are not promised that we will reap *where* we sow.

My company recently did a $70,000 home improvement project for a customer even though our quote was higher than that of the other bidder. Why? The customer told me that, a couple of years earlier, we had done a small repair on his home, and, as it had turned out to be a quick repair, we had not charged him. Because of that, he preferred to use us now. It all comes back.

By the way, the repairman who did not charge him for the work took that action on his own. That is the type of employee you should be looking for.

Another incident occurred when the metro Atlanta area experienced a deluge of rain so severe that it was one of the lead stories for several days on the national evening news. A customer for whom we had earlier done a small roof repair had the leak return and called our office during the storms—twice, but never received a return call. In the maelstrom of frantic phone calls for help we were receiving, for some reason, her calls had not been dispatched. She finally hired someone else to repair the leak.

On her third call to our office, almost one month after the first call for help, she reached me to let me know what had happened and how disappointed she was. After I verified her story and discovered our error, I apologized sincerely and refunded the money she had originally spent with us, without her ever requesting it.

I also assured her that, despite the full refund, her warranty on the area we had repaired for her would be honored if the need arose in the future, even though someone else had performed the corrective work. Her last words to me were, "I picked your company because of your reputation, but thought I had made a mistake. I see now why your company has the reputation in Atlanta that it does. We need these ethics in every business, everywhere, every day. Thank you."

Which contractor do you think will get her future business? And isn't it likely she will tell two or three other people about that unusual experience? Probably.

But I did not do it for those reasons. In fact, *those reasons never crossed my mind*. I did it because it was the right thing to do—plus a little. If I had been in her position and she had been in mine, that is how I would have wanted to be treated, plus a little.

It was the Golden Rule being applied in real life. Had I been in her place that would have "wowed" me. What would I wish done if I were the other party? That is always the solution I look for. Then, I try to add a little.

However, in those unusual instances when the other party is being unreasonable, I do stand my ground. That too is Golden Rule conduct as well. There is no place in business for pushovers, and there shouldn't be for dishonest customers, either.

When I am dealing with a customer who is being unreasonable—rare because of our strict attention to the screening of customers and projects—I am just as quick to defend my company or my employees, and with as much respectful vigor as the customer makes necessary. I do not allow disrespect

TEN BUSINESS GUIDELINES

toward any customer nor do I allow any action that fails to live up to the spirit of the contract, and I respectfully but firmly require the same of customers. As I said, the business world is no place for pushovers.

I am never afraid of any threats a customer may make because I always do voluntarily what a responsible business owner would be expected to do. As a result of the Golden Rule standard in my business, and our selective screening of projects/customers before bidding, no attorneys have ever been required to resolve any issue since I assumed control of the business thirty-one years ago. When we make a mistake, we fix it. And when a customer blusters for no justifiable reason, I have nothing to fear.

The Golden Rule is the God-given guide for prosperity in all dealings between parties of good will in business—and this includes not just customers, but also employees. It should be automatic to consider an employee's point of view.

As an example, just today one of my men made a mistake that cost my company $1,425 on a job he had sold. This man is one of my best and brightest workers. He was willing, and fully expecting, to pay the company back his commission. I called him and said, "I'm sure you won't make that mistake again. I'll look at the numbers and give you some help if I can."

After looking the job over, I called him back and told him, "I'll hold $425 out of your commission and I'll pay $1,000 of the loss myself. That way, neither of us will be hurt too badly, and you can get back to work with a clear mind."

I have another employee who does excellent work for our customers and has made money for both of us over the years. When I heard that his father was ill and he had to help cover some of his father's medical expenses, I sent him a check for $1,000 to help with the bills.

Another valuable long-term employee got into short-term financial trouble through no fault of his own. He needed a few thousand dollars. I told him, "I'll take a look at the jobs you do for me next week and pay you all the profits made on them until you get caught up."

Now, don't get the idea that I am a patsy. I can assure you that none of my employees have that misconception. I tell them when I hire them what is expected, and then I let them know, "If you fail to perform your duties or follow the rules here, I'll be coming. And it won't take three days for me to get around to it either."

It is precisely because I am *not* a weak leader or a soft touch that these proofs of appreciation and partnership are so effective. They know it is because I love them and admire them and appreciate what they do for me in my business. I actually tell them I love and appreciate them—because I do!

But don't try to pass counterfeit currency here. It has to be real, and it has to feel right coming from you in that moment. But it is not uncommon for me to end a conversation with one of my employees with, "Thank you. I love you and I appreciate what you are doing. I enjoy this business more because you are here." And, without any awkward feelings, they will say right back, "I love you, too, man. And I love working here. Talk to you later." And they mean it.

The employees who create their own trouble or have not yet proven their commitment to my business would not get the same response from me. Although not all the men and women I hire make the team, the ones who do truly enjoy working for me. I know because they tell me.

I ask my employees to rise to the highest level of professionalism. When they do, I admire them for their skill, I respect them for their diligence, and, yes, I love them for it and tell them so. When that is true—when it is really in your heart—you will know when it is appropriate to say so.

In the past many years, I have had only two employees leave my company voluntarily, and, within a year, one asked if he could return. I welcomed him back—everyone has the right to see if the grass is greener somewhere else, once—and today he is one of the most loyal employees I have. And that retention level is in an industry known for a high turnover rate. Of course, happy and contented employees result in happy customers, and this makes life much easier for everyone, especially me.

If you sign the checks, being the boss is your rightful position. But being the leader is not a decision you get to make. That esteemed position can only be granted to you from the men and women you direct.

If you want to become an industry leader, then you first need to earn the right to be the leader inside your own business. That comes from living the Golden Rule—with customers *and* employees.

When your goal is to build a business that is not only successful but will also give you a satisfactory lifestyle; you need to build an organization that delivers services in a fluid manner. This should be done with the highest standards of ethics and quality but without your direct involvement.

These ten guidelines made it possible for me to enjoy the business that I built, and they can do the same for you. But nothing will work long-term unless you take seriously my suggestion that you price your product or service to make a true profit. In the next chapter, I will share some thoughts on how to lead your business into that essential measure of success.

CHAPTER 4
THE 80/20 RULE

"All we ever do is work long hours and 'turn money,' but not much of it is ours!"

In any line of work, it is generally true that eighty percent of the businesses make only twenty percent of the profits—which means that two out of ten businesses are splitting eighty percent of the money being made. That difference in income is staggering.

Why does this occur? There can be numerous reasons, the most obvious being a lack of ability in the people running the less-successful businesses. However, in my opinion, very near the top of the list would be a too-frequent willingness to sell for too little money in order to generate business.

The Problem of Pricing

If you offer a product or service to the marketplace and a customer gives you their business, integrity requires that you fulfill every commitment made in a professional manner. Fairness also requires that the men and women who perform the tasks be fairly compensated. And good business practice requires that you meet every obligation on time to the creditors and vendors that supply your business.

But is it not equally clear that *you* should receive appropriate payment after all direct and indirect expenses for supplying the need of the purchaser?

Fairness to your family requires that *you* be fairly compensated, too. It is as much an injustice to underpay your self as it is to overcharge a customer or to shortchange your hardworking employees.

So, to put it plainly, a well-run business is not run by "turning your money" (using current receipts to pay overdue bills). Your product must be priced to cover all direct and indirect expenses, on time, with a little extra to set aside for future contingencies, and still pay yourself a fair return for your labors.

My business is not large enough to need a full-time financial officer. But there are persons that teach how to calculate over-head accurately and set the correct price for doing businesses, and for far less than the information is worth.

If you fail to price your service properly, you will eventually be forced to "short one to cover another;" and that is a slippery slope. Businesses that start down that path either remain in, or are soon relegated to, the lower eighty percent that are fighting each other over only twenty percent of the money made in that line of work. What other outcomes could possibly result from selling too cheaply?

The range from the worst to the best in quality in my business is almost never more than twenty percent and usually closer to ten. That is probably true for many other businesses. Those few points make all the difference. There is some percentage of every population that understands you can't get something for nothing, and those are the customers you want to work for. Happily, I have also found those same people are the best type of customer to work for, as they have the most reasonable expectations, appreciate a job well-done, and are prompt to pay.

> *The only way I know to run a business*
> *that delivers satisfaction all the way around*
> *is to charge what it costs,*
> *work for the people willing to pay it,*
> *and then see to it that you meet or exceed expectations.*

The methods may change a bit for each type of business, but my point, if broadly considered, would benefit a great many struggling entrepreneurs.

Real profits allow us to feel good about our chosen vocation and ourselves. Profits make us feel that our work is justified and valued in the marketplace. Working for little money would make anyone discouraged—and eventually, disgusted with themself. If we are going to work, we need to be paid. I would rather take the day off than spend it working for no money.

Last month I conducted a job interview with a man who used to own a large roofing company. For years, all I heard about was what a great business he had; then I heard he had suddenly gone out of business. When we met to discuss the possibility of him working for me, I said, "You ran a business much like this. How did you price your jobs there?"

He said, "I tried to get the actual overhead and make a ten percent profit for the company, plus get a little more than that for myself, but I couldn't sell at those prices."

"So, what did you do?" I asked.

"I went to the prices everybody seemed to be charging so I could sell more jobs."

I said, "I understand. I have seen that done many times. How did it work out for you?"

He told me, "I did a lot more business. But, two years later I hit a rough patch, and I had nothing to get through it with. I just had to fold."

I said, "I'm sorry to hear that. Frustrating and tiring, wasn't it? I used to do the same thing, but I don't anymore. I charge what I have to in order to make an honest profit, a *real* one after all my direct and indirect expenses. I decided that, if I wasn't really being paid, there was no reason to be working."

Don't assume from this that I am saying that we must get paid as much as we would like, or we think we should. I often have to sell for less than I think is an ideal exchange, but I never compete based solely on price, and I never knowingly sell for less than true overhead, with a real profit for the company, and then some left for me.

Working hard while hardly earning enough to prosper will eventually wear down anyone, financially and emotionally. Don't do it.

Outgo Matters, Too

Pricing of your product or service is indeed critical, but a business also needs to watch its outgo in order to be successful. Let me offer some hard-won advice in this area, too.

Stay current with your billing cycles. Do not slip into paying past bills with current business activity. A lot of small businesses do that, but, if you run yours that way, you are going to have serious pressures quickly if anything goes wrong.

Don't let your company assume so much debt that business has to be stronger than normal for you to meet the obligations easily. If you do, here's the solution: pay it off *and* find a way to operate without so many financed assets.

Watch your advertising costs like a hawk. Are they giving you enough real profit to justify the expense? In most cases, an expensive advertising budget only succeeds in making the small business owner an indentured servant to the advertiser's accounts receivable department. I require that my advertising dollars return five times what was spent. If it doesn't, I drop it. They don't get to fool me twice.

A happy customer is the least expensive and the most effective form of advertisement. When choosing to advertise, negotiate for short-term trials. Get introductory pricing for the first month to allow you to validate their claims. If that's not acceptable to them, you might want to wait. I have rarely found claims by advertisers reliable. And I found out early on that I really resented working just to pay the ad costs.

Now we come to an area of expense over which you have complete control: the amount you take out of your business to pay yourself. Until you have all bills paid with a cushion left in the operating account and have a fully funded backup account for customer service, delayed receivables, and unexpected expenses, you should keep the amount of money you take out of the business to live on to a minimum.

This may require a few years of sacrifice, but it is more than worth it in the long run. For many years now, very little that has happened in my business that has caused me any great stress because I have either already made provision for it or have the reserves to cover it.

Let me share one more thought on spending for advertising and general caution in business. Many new business owners start out wanting to grow rapidly right from the start. My experience is this: that which grows gradually behaves best.

You Have to Make a Real Profit

I know nothing about how to run a Fortune 500 company, and I am sure the rules are very different. But I am writing to the new entrepreneur, the entry-level CEO, and most businesses, even when successful, will have fewer than one hundred employees, most fewer than fifty. There are millions of such companies and too many have constant cash flow problems. The owners fear they will not stay in business if they charge what they need to in order to deliver a quality product and pay themselves a fair return. In truth, this happens in many larger companies. Anytime a business depends on being one of the cheapest providers, safety, compensation, and training will get squeezed out.

And this is literally dangerous. Why? There are many reasons. But the problem that I have seen too often is that the owner will be too busy working hard to realize they are not getting anywhere. It is actually hard to see that when you are very busy. And they remain in that state for years until they lose their business due to some unexpected event, or their health, or their family.

Sadly, a few years ago, I got a call informing me that one of my biggest competitors had taken their own life. I had long suspected, from looking at the prices that company quoted, that there had to be money problems there. I asked someone familiar with the facts if they knew the reason for this tragic incident. I was told that though there may have been other issues, the money problems were definitely a big factor. I was so saddened to even hear of the event. I knew how hard and how many years that man had worked. He just eventually used up the vigor, the very life, that was at one time inside himself. And he did millions in sales.

Listen to me, reader: if you decide to start a business, it is far better to do $1,000,000 a year profitably than ten times that much while accomplishing little more than "turning money" and using up your life.

I recently treated two of my main suppliers to a nice dinner out in Atlanta. Of course, usually, they are the ones treating me, but I wanted to show my appreciation and give my helpful account reps a great meal. During the dinner, they commented on how valued my account was. I said I appreciated that, but I knew that a lot of their customers were much bigger. Without mentioning any names, one of them said, "True, but don't be fooled. We just cut off a twenty-million-dollar account for non-payments." Size and sales volume are nothing to be proud of when your suppliers aren't getting paid. And volume will provide no lasting protection from violating the profit rule.

Here is what the 80/20 rule tells me as a business owner:

> *The only men and women accomplishing their goal of being a successful business owner with a satisfactory lifestyle who provides quality results for happy customers—are the few in that top 20 percent.*

And this is where the rewards for being in business—financial and emotional—are to be found.

I wasn't born smarter than the next guy. I learned all this the hard way. My stepfather repeatedly told me, "Price sells. As long as we are turning our money, we will be okay." But we were not okay. After more than a decade of that, I told Frank, "All we ever do is work long hours and 'turn money,' but not much of it is ours!"

I worked much too long letting my cheapest competitors set *my* prices. After many exhausting years, dismal beyond the telling, I finally decided that if I couldn't get paid a fair wage for doing what I was doing, I would find something else to do.

What I discovered was, in fact, it had been up to me all along how I would run my own business. The professionalism of my business improved, and the customer satisfaction rate, and sales and real income, all began to climb.

Remember this:

> *No amount of success is more important to your happiness than your relationship with God, time with family, and your health. More money is never worth your family, your mental or physical health, or your soul.*

Yes, building a business is a demanding task. It is not for everyone. In fact, it is so demanding that it can and will, and on many occasions must, crowd out other very important things.

For the first ten years or so, it may be impossible to build the business and have as much time for family as you would prefer. But that time frame must be limited, or the price becomes too high. Your business model must take the needs of health and family—and aging and time—into account. Price accordingly.

Many years ago, when I was still selling jobs myself, if a customer questioned my price I would say something like, "I enjoy what I do and I am going to do a good job for you. But in order for me to do this I have to be able to make a living at it. If you hire my company, we are going to do exactly what we promised and we will be here for you if there is ever a need. I know that price is a big consideration. It is for all of us. So I priced this as competitively as I could and still accomplish the one thing more important, and that is to always do the work well and to stay in business."

In a foot race, the prize will go to the fastest. But in life, consistency in a sound plan is a great equalizer. It will allow you to finish very close to the super-talented.

Let your sound plan be based on fair dealings and enough profit to justify your efforts. Do the right things with the money when you earn it. Instead of pulling the money out of the company and piling up more personal obligations with it, take care of the business first. Then you will remain able to operate on the profitable side of the 80/20 rule. It is pressure to raise money to cover bills that gets a business in trouble. (For more on this important subject of the proper use of time and money, you might want to read my first book in this series, *Riches Beyond the Bling*.)

CHAPTER 5
SHREWDNESS IN BUSINESS

In the affairs of this world, men are saved not by faith, but by the want of it.

—Benjamin Franklin

Here is some important material on caution and self-protection that will prove helpful to you in business and in your private life. This is hard-won; I have learned only through experience that a certain degree of shrewdness is a required virtue in what is indeed a designing world.

Over the last thirty-plus years I have read and reread more than two hundred carefully selected books in order to gain a little judgment about this world. Would you like to know the most important sentence I have ever read on the subject of business or money? All right, I will tell you. The most instructive single sentence on business I have ever read is this:

You can lose a fortune believing in the pledged word or promised intentions.

SHREWDNESS IN BUSINESS

Unfortunately, I do not remember where I read that or who wrote it; it has been too many years ago.

Thousands of years before you or I were born, the Bible's book of Proverbs pronounced this same warning: "Only simpletons believe everything they're told! The prudent carefully consider their steps." (14:15, New Living Translation)

Reliably, you can put promises, good intentions, and earnest assurances at the top of the list of the most cheaply traded things you will deal with in business and in this life.

I long followed the late financial writer Richard Russell. He wrote *Dow Theory Letters*, a regular interpretation of the financial markets (now carried on by Aden Research). From 1958 until nearly the day of his death in November 2015, Mr. Russell wrote regularly on the subject of money and investing. Over 14,000 people around the world subscribed to his internet newsletter. He was no fool.

Mr. Russell wrote that, after more than eighty years of living, he had concluded that one of the hardest things in the world to do was to find someone who will do exactly what they say they will do. The second hardest thing, he stated, was to find out what the truth is and what the objective facts really are any time money is involved.

Don't Be a Patsy

When it comes to business, you simply cannot afford to rely on assurances. So, to avoid being a patsy, the first and most important rule is this:

> *Do not make business decisions based on statistical claims, pledges, or intentions.*

Protect yourself first and be assertive about it. Require that all important stipulations and requirements are placed in a written agreement and make payments contingent on performance. Do not put money on the table without protections in place.

I will give you three words you would do well to memorize right now:

Everything is negotiable.

And I do mean *everything*. Those two thoughts, do not make decisions based on promises and everything can be negotiated, are the fountainhead of shrewdness. Never accept any plan where "they" have your money and all you have are their assurances, promises, and claims.

Let me share with you an example from my own industry to illustrate this point perfectly. When a parent at my daughter's karate studio found out I was in the home improvement business, he remarked that he had just lost $6,000 to a dishonest roofing company. I asked him what happened.

He said,

> *Someone knocked on my door and told me they were in the neighborhood replacing roofs due to a storm that had passed through the area. He offered to look over my roof for free while he was there. Afterward, he told me I had storm damage and that he could help me get a new roof for free from my homeowners' insurance. I told him to go ahead, and I actually got a $6,000 check as a partial settlement, the remainder to be paid when the roof was replaced.*

> *I signed a contract for him to do the roof and he took the insurance check as a deposit. He said that was the way everyone did it, and that I had his signed contract, which legally obligated him to doing the work. He seemed very nice and professional, but I never heard from him again. The phone number on the contract is now disconnected.*

That particular company was one I was familiar with. They had closed up shop with the checks of more than 6,600 Georgia homeowners in their bank accounts in the Caribbean, but very few roofs were ever installed, and those few were of dubious quality, no doubt. The state attorney general is after them now, but I doubt any of the victims will ever see their money again.

Every one of these homeowners gave a stranger who knocked on their door thousands of dollars in exchange for an official-looking piece of paper called a "contract" that cost the crooks only pennies to print! Six thousand six hundred victims from that one company alone. All any of these gullible people had to do was refuse to give anyone any money until they had a new roof on their home.

Instead, they let themselves be led down a path of folly by a convincing storyteller—and their own desire to get something for nothing. Remember this: hustles always start when the "mark" has accepted the "setup" after a seemingly helpful and sincere *unsolicited* contact. The hustler gets them to part with real money while all he has given them in return is promises and a few words written on a piece of paper that cost him less than a dime.

Another acquaintance of mine called to ask what I thought of a $50,000 investment he was considering. He wanted to bring in a company to make his business more profitable and organized. I told him to instead join a business association that represented his industry and attend the events they scheduled.

I encouraged him to develop some acquaintances in his industry that were distant enough that their respective companies would never compete, and then start talking to and helping each other. That approach is free and life-enriching, as true friendships can come from it, and there is no cost or private motive behind the relationship.

At a minimum, I suggested, if he hired a company to make his business more profitable, he should make payment contingent on measurable results. I even offered to come by and see if I could help him myself.

I saw him a year later. In passing, he mentioned that he had hired and paid the "experts at efficiency and profit" company because the "proofs" of their claims had been so convincing—and that he now had nothing to show for it. Indeed, they were now telling him his complaints were unwarranted and he was being unreasonable; after all, results take a little time to show up on bank statements and he should have understood that when he signed up.

The truth? They are taking their families on vacation this year with his money—and he is not taking his family on vacation this year because they have his money.

Here is another real-life lesson. A little more than a year ago, a friend's house burned down. When he received the settlement check to rebuild his house, a settlement company representative who had acted as a go-between for my friend and his home insurance company, suggested he call a "wonderful builder" who did "all the restoration work for our clients." So, my friend asked my opinion on how to proceed.

I suggested he take the check, talk to some reputable contractors I knew, and hire his own builder. I said, "There is no reason to hire a builder you don't know anything about just because he was recommended by someone else you don't really know anything about at the settlement company."

He told me again about all the assurances the nice lady at the settlement company had given him. I made my point again. (Silly me.) He once again repeated with confidence the assurances given about the quality of this builder by someone at the settlement company. He hired the contractor.

Well, as I said, it has now been over a year—and he is no closer to having his home rebuilt. I don't think he has seen that builder more than three times, although he does occasionally have some very angry employees come by looking for the "home builder" who owes them money.

Much of what has been done will have to be redone, and $90,000 of his settlement money is now in the pocket of the "wonderful builder" who is evidently so wealthy that he does not find it necessary to show up at work.

I can tell you after speaking with him myself that he is a very agreeable man and always ready to "get all this taken care of starting tomorrow!" Tomorrow is evidently the only day he works.

And what about the nice lady whose assurances and words dripping with goodwill and sympathy won my friend's trust? She dismisses any complaints about her builder friend (or whatever he really is to her: someone giving her kickbacks or maybe a relative?) as coming from some irrational customer: "Why are you so upset? He's on it! So, you're living in a rented apartment with no air conditioning and sleeping on the couch. That's to be expected when things like this happen. He's only six months behind schedule. He'll get it done. Give the guy a chance! And don't call me with any more of these silly complaints!"

> The first precept was never to accept a thing as true until I knew it as such without a single doubt.
> —René Descartes

The point is this: taking suggestions from someone when the other person could have an unknown personal motive is risky.

If someone approaches you and suggests someone you should use, and especially if they were not asked and seem intent on convincing you to listen to them, you might be wise to find whatever you need elsewhere. Remember: almost all hustles start with a seemingly helpful *unsolicited contact*.

In fairness to my friend, I do not fault him. It is almost impossible to enter a business arrangement without the final judgment eventually coming down to a decision to trust the other party. However, there are a few additional precautions I would like to suggest, particularly when the decision involves a considerable amount of money.

Beware the Unsolicited Contact

I've said this before, and I will say it again and again:

> *Be very skeptical about doing business with someone who solicits you first.*

Investing money as a result of an unsolicited call from a stockbroker, buying an expensive product from someone who knocks on your door, or going through with any other similar act is just plain foolish—there is simply no other way to put it.

Let me give you an example of a relatively harmless solicitation, one I refused just last week. I had a problem with my cell phone, so I went to the company's local sales and service office. While I was waiting for a technician to see me, a pleasant young lady approached me with a big smile and asked how I was doing and if I had been served (not out of sincere interest—this was a sales approach icebreaker).

She then asked who had the internet service at my home and asked for my home telephone number, explaining that her company had a new program designed to lower my rates. I declined to give her my number. She questioned whether I had heard her correctly. I told her I had. She persisted. If I just gave her some personal information, she explained, she was going to save me money. I declined again.

She became a little more determined, the smile replaced by a look of irritation. I politely declined again. After a minute spent questioning me as to why I wouldn't give her personal information not related to my visit, someone else walked in, and she went after them. (By the way, she signed them up.) My cell phone was repaired a few minutes later and I left.

SHREWDNESS IN BUSINESS

I was not offended by this young lady's actions or by my cell phone company's planned solicitation of me—perhaps better described as the ambush of a captive audience. If I were a shareholder in that company, I still would have declined the offer but been quite pleased with what they were doing.

Now, let's analyze what really happened:

1. I did not initiate the contact.

2. To bundle all my services, as the young woman wanted me to do, I would have had to sign forms crammed with language ten attorneys could not have explained to me—or her.

3. Since I am happy with what I have now, only a naïve something-for-nothing hope on my part could have induced me into the deal. (The management that put this program in place knows that part of human nature well and built it into the sales approach.)

4. I would not likely have actually spent less once I accepted all the "great upgrades" presented as "additional wise and valuable choices"—*after* I had signed the first agreement, of course.

5. This woman was paid by the hour, or on commission, and needed sales to keep her job. She knew little more about what she was selling than I did. She is a responsible young lady working to support herself—by getting people to sign papers that neither she nor they fully understand. The company was trying to hit its revenue growth projections for the stock analysts on Wall Street, and my checkbook was the oyster between the cats.

6. If this had been a deal I thought I might be interested in, I could easily have taken down the web

address and read it over at my leisure without answering any of her questions. Signing up on the spot would have required me to violate the one rule I hope I never violate: I do not do business with anyone who solicits me first. If I had decided to participate after reviewing the information at my leisure, I could easily have done so at a later time.

Admittedly, this whole scenario required only a minor decision, but this is exactly how costly mistakes get started in business—by entertaining *any* conversation initiated by someone unfamiliar to you concerning your business or your money.

Unfortunately, I haven't always been so cautious. About thirty years ago, someone knocked at the door of my business and asked if I needed the parking area in the back of my office blacktopped. The pleasant stranger explained that they had just finished a nearby paving job and had a full load of unused asphalt leftover, asphalt paid for by the previous customer. I could get the materials for free and the labor for a bargain price if I gave them permission to go to work right away so the asphalt could be used while it was still warm. They did not want to drive all the way across town just to dump it.

I did have an area that needed surfacing, and I took the bait. The newly paved area looked beautiful—for two weeks. Within a few months it was so broken up I had to pay to have it removed.

I later found out these people were making their way across the state doing work so poorly that it barely lasted until the checks cleared the bank. Their story of "leftover asphalt" was the setup for the scam. They bought a truckload of asphalt *and then went looking for an idiot to sell it to.* (I must have looked like their guy.) They knew the common weakness of us all. We all want to think we can get something for nothing. I was $4,000 poorer and a lot wiser.

I should have known better. When I was a policeman, offenses ranging from property crimes to murder occurred after naïve homeowners' hired friendly strangers who knocked on their door offering to perform some service for them.

If you need a yardman or a roof or an investment or a business deal, *you* do the research and initiate the contact. If you are solicited by a stranger calling you on the telephone or knocking on your door or initiating contact with you while out in public, and you take the bait, *your odds of being in proficient and honest hands are almost zero.* This is one of the few rules you can safely say there are no justifiable exceptions.

Here is some instructive advice you should stamp indelibly into your mind for any decision-making process involving money:

> *Good business deals never go begging for money. They are kept away from the public.*

Get Legal Advice Before Making Any Commitment

If a good bit of money is involved, use an attorney to look over whatever you are considering. What you are *not* seeing and what you don't even know to ask about can hurt you—a lot!

Consult a lawyer because you can't ask the right questions when you don't even know what you don't know. And *after* you create problems for yourself is the wrong time to find out just how much you didn't know.

Let me give you an example. A friend of mine decided to buy a modest home for her daughter. She had the deed to the home placed in her daughter's name, assuming that putting the deed in her name alone would protect her daughter's ownership of the home in the event of a divorce.

A few years later, her daughter and son-in-law did, in fact, decide to divorce. It was only then that the mother discovered, in that state, the laws were such that her son-in-law did not need to have one dime of his own money invested in the home, nor did his name need to appear on the deed, for him to be entitled to claims on the home in the event of divorce. In the eyes of the law, if they both lived in it, regardless of who owned it, he had an equitable interest in the home.

One phone call to an attorney *before* anything was done, back when the home was purchased, would have allowed for a more satisfactory arrangement to be made. Fortunately, in this case, the son-in-law did the honorable thing and declined his equitable interest. But that won't happen often.

Remember this: on important matters, the time to talk to an attorney is *before* you sign the contract. The time to talk to a mentor or other advisor is *before* you make a commitment or part with any money.

Of course, if the expense is small, you may decide—and rightly so—just to use your own judgment to save time. But when the dollar amounts are significant, don't rely on your own judgment, particularly if you are unfamiliar with the legal documents or issues involved.

Accepting superficial verbal explanations of binding legal documents is naïve. The other party will always have an interest in the deal being made on the best terms possible for them. So get legal counsel *before* you commit yourself. And be willing to pay for it because it could turn out to be the smartest money you ever spent.

Persuasiveness and a reassuringly sincere personality are the stock-in-trade of the incompetent and the crook. Sincerity is one of the easiest things in the world to counterfeit if one wishes to dupe another person. The longer someone does it, the better he or she gets at it. It is always safest to assume there are unknown issues that warrant seeking professional legal counsel whenever significant amounts of money are involved.

One more time: if you are going to build a house or do anything else of significance, have an attorney *familiar with that legal specialty* look over the agreement between you and the other party before signing.

That person should read over all agreements and then counsel you on protective clauses you should add, or problematic conditions or clauses you should remove or modify. Ask your lawyer to look for anything that could be a problem. Everything can be negotiated, and that includes the terms the other party says cannot be changed. Have your attorney strike any clauses, write in any stipulations, or make other amendments needed to protect your interests.

Remember this: a shrewd man or woman pays an attorney a little money to avoid trouble in the first place. The fool pays an attorney a lot of money to try to get out of trouble after he or she is in it. *But both pay the attorney.* Be the smart one. Save yourself a lot of money. Pay them first.

Use the Best Professionals

We've been talking about hiring the right kind of attorney, but that may involve more than just choosing someone out of the phone book or off the Internet. If the dollar amounts involved are large, you want the one of the *best* attorneys, because you want the best counsel possible in important business or personal legal matters.

When I needed a real estate attorney, I didn't call around to see who was the cheapest. After securing a line of credit and having a general conversation with my banker about my intentions, I asked a bank executive who has been financing real estate in the county for twenty years, "Which would be the best law firm to help me learn the business from an investment point of view and guide me in how to protect my interests?" A firm and a name were suggested.

Similarly, if I needed a mortgage broker, I wouldn't ask my neighbor. I would ask the real estate attorney connected with that law firm for a referral. Who would know mortgage brokers better than one of the most successful real estate attorneys in the county, one who had been closing local real estate deals for years?

A referral is no better than the person making it.

The branch manager of your bank is a great resource. He or she will know people successfully involved in just about anything you are considering. Paying top-tier attorneys, accountants, tax consultants, and estate planning experts is an appropriate, necessary, and *willingly paid* expense for the savvy man or woman of business. And, as you begin to rise in the world, it is an expense you should seek out rather than attempt to avoid.

> No man is wise enough by himself.
> —Titus Maccius Plautus

Never Buy During the Glitter Show

More shrewd advice: never decide to make a purchase or sign any papers during what I call the "glitter show."

Organized sales pitches can be very convincing. And there is nothing wrong with sales pitches. Every legitimate product in the world has to have a marketing plan.

A good sales plan attempts to prevent hesitancy by creating such a compelling situation that a decision is made while emotions are still running high.

But right after the glitter show is not the right time for you to make a commitment. You will need some time after the initial burst of enthusiasm has waned to be sure this offer is everything it was presented to be and something you really need and can afford. Wait a few days, or a week, and then sit down with your spouse and talk it through.

Don't ever do business with anyone who tells you the decision has to be made now or the opportunity will be withdrawn or that the price is a "special opportunity" or a "one-time-only offer" and the price will be increased if you wait to think it over. Don't debate it; leave—running.

Trust me. They want you to sign papers or write a check while your rational perspective is pushed into the background, and that is exactly the kind of decision that usually leads to regret. Do you really think they won't take your money for the same terms if you wait to consider the deal first? Not likely.

So, do not accept pressure in any form to make a significant financial decision on the spot. After all, such pressure is usually an indicator that what they wish you to agree to is very good for them and not such a good deal for you.

If you are conducting business and someone attempts to force you to decide in favor of their proposition, tell them this: "If I truly have to make a decision right now, then my answer is definitely no. I have a rule I have followed for years and it is this: I never make a decision to spend or invest money without time to think it through. I permit myself no exceptions to that rule—ever—and I have never regretted following it, and it is not likely that I will regret it this time. But even if I do, I will not be forced to decide now."

This may be more direct than you are comfortable with but get some grit and stand up for yourself. If you are being pressured, then you are being treated like a mark in a shell game.

I have dealt with attorneys, bankers, accountants, insurance agents, and suppliers in legitimate business matters for years, and an honest professional has never pressured me. *Not once.* If someone is pressuring you to make a particular decision, then you are either being asked to agree to a deal you probably do not need or you are dealing with the wrong people to get financially entangled with anyway.

I talked about this earlier in terms of hiring, but the principle carries into all business relationships: I suggest you never enter into business with anyone who—without being asked about it—drops hints about their religious convictions as support for their claim of being trustworthy. To some of you this warning may seem prejudicial against kindly people, but I urge you to trust me here, this kind of approach is often a reliable indicator of future trouble. If you doubt it then do as you wish. You can judge for yourself after you have lived a while.

> Avoid, as you would the plague, a clergyman who is also a man of business.
> —Saint Jerome

I was interviewing a man a few years ago when he said, "I'm a Christian. That's the way I do business. I hope that is all right with you." His comment was out of place in the conversation we were having. He just interjected it, as if it should set my mind at ease so I would hire him. It did not.

My experience has been that someone who uses their religion to be a credit to *them*, instead of living their life in such a way that they are credit to their faith even when nothing is said, are, shall we say, an unfinished work in character? And after being around some of them during my years of living, I think it likely that more than a few of them wouldn't know God if He came down in person and bit them on the leg.

Three More Ways to Be Shrewd

My cautionary tales could go on, but let me share with you three more quick bits of advice about being properly cautious before we leave this chapter.

1. *Once you have assets to protect, consider purchasing an umbrella insurance policy.* I have a friend who is a physician, and he related to me this incident of a shocking loss. A friend of his, also a physician, needed his house painted. A young man in the neighborhood—the local high school football hero and a really nice kid—asked if he could do the painting as he needed the money to get ready for college, and, of course, the doctor kindly agreed.

The kid fell from a ladder and was paralyzed for life. The eventual judgment far exceeded the $1,000,000 of liability the doctor had on his homeowner's policy and the good doctor was financially ruined. Scary stuff!

I dodged a crisis of my own when one of my daughter's horses escaped from the pasture after a tree downed a section of fence. The animal walked onto the nearby highway and was hit by two vehicles. Both cars had multiple occupants, and the damage to both vehicles was severe. Amazingly, no one was hurt, and even the horse survived and recovered. Had there been fatalities, besides the terrible remorse, the costs could have greatly exceeded even a million dollars in homeowners liability insurance, which is why I carry a multi-million dollar umbrella policy over my assets.

Use insured professionals to work on your property when any potential danger is involved. Carry insurance policies large enough to cover you in event of need. Buy an umbrella policy for extra coverage when your assets justify it. This type of insurance is not expensive.

And, once you are worth a good bit of money, keep your various assets—home, investment accounts, and so on—held by separate entities so they are kept apart from each other. Then your entire estate is not up for grabs due to one lawsuit leveled against you. This is not expensive or complicated to arrange; any asset protection attorney familiar with the laws specific to your state or country can help with this.

2. *With the exception of a car loan, avoid credit contracts.* Most really serious, long-term, high-cost mistakes involve contracts obligating you to payments. They are almost impossible to escape once you are in them.

After watching a commercial last week, my daughter asked me, "Dad, what is interest?" I told her, "It is the cost to use someone else's money to buy something you can't afford yet."

This same caution would apply to advertising agreements for your business. Most advertisers want you to sign a contract for an extended period of time. These should be modified so you are not stuck for a year with expensive obligations that might fail to deliver the promised benefits. If an advertiser will not agree to a short-term trial, it might be best to wait until you can find a way to accomplish your goals without giving up a big part of your cash flow to a sales rep trying to make their own next car payment.

3. *You can't afford to wait a single day to act on the threat of identity theft.* You must be proactive to minimize the risk of this crime.

Identity theft is the fastest-growing criminal activity in the world. The deceits and scams are varied and beyond our ability to protect ourselves from completely. So, it is imperative that, if you do not know how to put safeguards in place for yourself, you pay a small monthly fee for the services of an identity theft protection company.

And obviously, as a first line of defense, never reveal personal information of any sort to anyone who requests such information by email, phone, or in-person until you have personally confirmed their legitimacy and the need for the information by separate and independent means.

Variations of human deceit—legal and illegal—are ever-present realities in human affairs. These suggestions on how to act with shrewdness in a designing world are not exhaustive or foolproof but following them may spare you from costly distress.

Successful men and women of business are neither gullible nor naïve, and to the extent possible they protect themselves ahead of need.

CHAPTER 6

DO YOU HAVE A DESIRE TO WORK FOR YOURSELF?

Is becoming an entry-level CEO for you? Perhaps a quick summary of some of what we've learned about being a successful business owner will help you decide.

Let's Recap

There is a difference between owning your own job and owning a business. The objective in building a business of your own is to make your direct involvement in the day-to-day routine unnecessary for it to run smoothly and produce income, the exception being any time there are unusual difficulties within the business or much higher than normal business activity.

That requires talented associates, which in turn requires that the business charge the customer enough to deliver efficient, delegated service. The cheapest competitor cannot possibly be the yardstick for pricing, either to a rational business owner or to customers seeking honest value for their money.

However, men and women who start their own businesses are commonly afraid to charge the few additional percentage points required to deliver a truly superior product and experience. As a result, they grind out a problematic living while dealing with building resentments and overtaxed emotions.

The one non-negotiable skill every man or woman in business needs is the ability to discern men and women of character, work ethic, and skills appropriate to the task—and then put them to work in the area of their strength. When it comes to your workforce, don't try to force square pegs into round holes. Hire talented people, delegate everything possible to them, and keep them doing the tasks they are good at.

Train your people and then monitor their performance—correct right away, praise right away. Keep them working in the areas of their strengths and when possible protect them from assignments which irritate them and for which they are poorly suited.

Create a culture in which everyone is respected, and good work and initiative are acknowledged and rewarded.

A properly managed business is evidenced by fluidity. Removing any impediments to efficiency and harmonious cooperation should be a top priority. Any employee, any customer, or any work activity that brings friction into your business should be removed, modified, or avoided in the future. Do not tolerate sand in the machine.

A business is not capable of maximum profits until it is nearly frictionless. I am not saying a business can be run problem-free, but the same problems should not be happening repeatedly. Solving *other* people's problems in a fluid manner and for a fair profit is the description of a well-run business.

Train everyone in the organization to run toward problems, not from them. That includes you—handle the tough ones yourself.

As far as possible, make everything about doing business with you a "Disney quality" experience.

Communicate with the customer. Once an agreement to do business has been entered into, the communication with the customer should be thorough enough that calls from customers asking questions are rare.

DO YOU HAVE A DESIRE TO WORK FOR YOURSELF?

The business experience you provide to your customers should meet or exceed every reasonable expectation. It is important to have a filtering process for identifying and avoiding unreasonable customers and less than desirable business projects.

Decline any work that does not fit your personnel or the personality of your business. Let your competitors have the problem jobs and the problem people. Avoid imperious, strident customers. The profits from working for these people—if you ever get paid—are never worth the headache.

It cannot be overstated how important it is to know what to stay away from. Let your competitors' emotions and business resources be tied up with problems from taking the wrong jobs and working for the wrong people, not yours.

In matters of honest dispute, with the weight of valid points of disagreement approximately equal on either side, yield to the customer's viewpoint. However, when someone is attempting to bully you to get more service than they paid for or inventing dissatisfactions in order to pay less money than they owe, stand up and protect your business.

Don't cringe before bullies. Defend your employees and your company from unfounded complaints and do so in a straightforward manner without apology. When necessary, get involved and put yourself between your employee and an irascible client.

Many things may contribute to your success, but success is *determined* by becoming one of the best at what you do, rendering service in sufficient quantity, and receiving just compensation for that service.

I say it again: small business owners often sacrifice being paid fairly in order to stay busy. They try to thrive by never losing a prospective customer and therefore cause their business many frustrations. Wrong methods cannot bring right results. My experience is that the customers that want the cheap deal are also the worst customers to deal with in attitude.

THE ENTRY-LEVEL CEO

This one is worth repeating again and again:

Good financial management, business or personal, can be summed up in one word
—MARGIN.

Set aside a little money every month. Keep building a cash reserve in a separate company savings account until it is sufficient to handle customer service issues and unexpected expenses. Draw on these funds when your receivables get out of step with large bills coming due. That happens in all businesses from time to time. You might choose to use your line of business credit in these instances, but always keep a separate "fallback" account in case of sudden need.

Finally, respond to all complaints—from customers *and* employees—with the Golden Rule in mind. Put yourself in their place and ask, "If I were in his position, what would I wish to be done?"

As we leave this subject I offer a few simple suggestions that help me in big ways every day:

Do not trust your memory. Keep a small personal recorder on you at all times to capture every important detail that will need to be attended to later. I prefer a small personal recorder in my shirt pocket to my phones record function. It's just quicker for me. But if you prefer to use your phone for this, fine. Just be sure you do not rely on memory. It will eventually fail you and at times that could be costly.

As the first order of business each day I listen to and take care of each entry recorded the previous day. This one idea will increase your efficiency and reduce stress significantly. Nothing being overlooked due to a lapse in memory or busyness prevents stressful events.

Try not to let the days schedule control your emotions, though it will happen to everyone at times. When it starts getting hectic, slow your mind and emotions *by slowing down your tempo when you speak.* When you start feeling frazzled, purposely slow everything down mentally by just five percent. Speaking slower forces calmer tones and mentally delaying reactions to incoming information by just five percent will work surprisingly well when you have the discipline to do it.

An entry-level CEO must learn the art of managing the demands of business "from within." When I feel anxiety or become impatient from busyness, I repeat these words to myself: *I have the bearing of one whose calm assurance is agreeably manifest.* Then I take a short pause and a few deep breaths. When I resume, I slow my speaking and slow down my reaction time to incoming information by five percent.

Do not respond in anger. When provoked let incoming calls go to voicemail! Keep your hands off the send button! Do not make angry phone calls or send texts or emails in a fit of temper. They will turn out wrong every time.

Do You Have What It Takes?

Every business is a reflection of its owner. If you can't keep an orderly culture within your business, then generating sustainable and satisfactory income will be more difficult. If you lack the ability to bring order and system to an enterprise, then it is imperative that you get assistance from someone who is organized and have them can come in and set up a system. The inability to produce an orderly culture is fatal to the growth of small businesses.

You must have the strength of will to keep going when you do not know the way forward.

You must learn that what you can do about a problem is what you can do about a problem. Once you have done what you can, trust the answer to come or the need to be met when it is needed; even if it is one that you cannot see now.

If you have worried about something for a good long while, a few months perhaps, and no solution becomes clear, let it go and move on. Set your attention on the things you can do something about right now. No business succeeds in a straight line. Life has a way of solving or supplying these questions when the solution is truly needed, and often without much input from you. Faith.

Build a team of people that do their job well and to a finish, who do not need you to hold their hand and do not need to call you constantly.

Here are five common reasons many small business owners struggle or fail:

- They are not organized.
- They fail to maintain a sufficient margin of cash in a separate account for contingencies.
- When times are good they overspend and overcommit for their personal lifestyle.
- They set self-defeating prices, mistaking sales for profits.
- They lack honesty and integrity in all they say and do.

And there are two more key abilities for successful small business owners I'd like to mention.

I recently read of a study conducted to determine the single habit most likely to lead to financial wellbeing. Which one habit do you think most signaled a life free from disorders of every kind and was also the greatest constant among the financially independent? I didn't guess it. I bet you won't either.

It is the habit of getting out of bed early in the morning. In other words, a better life starts with how you choose to spend your time, especially in the mornings. *Unchain Your Brain,* the next book in my Common Sense for a Prosperous Life series, discusses how you can identify and move toward that which is of importance to you. When your life has an emotionally concentrated focus, then personal habits and use of time will begin to shift forward automatically. When you start thinking with specific intention, even when you have no idea how to get there, you begin to change what you involuntarily dwell on mentally—and that changes everything else.

Speaking for myself, to be mentally and physically healthy, born a citizen of a free and prosperous nation—one for which people wait in line to have the chance I inherited by birth—and then attempt nothing out of the ordinary because I do not know how to get started or because I'm afraid the odds are too much against me, is unacceptable. As I heard Joyce Meyer (www.joycemeyer.org) say once on television, in her typical, no-nonsense fashion, "Sometimes you just have to learn to do it afraid."

If you are interested in how to keep moving through fears and discouragements and direct your life to a purpose, I hope you will read *Unchain Your Brain* and also *Private Choices, Public Power*, the last two books in my series. For the future entry-level CEO's, *Unchain Your Brain* may be particularly helpful. It includes a section in which I discuss how to keep the task of starting a business mentally manageable, rather than being stopped by your own doubts before you even start.

Then there's persistence. It took me from the age of twenty-one to the age of twenty-eight before a legitimate opportunity was presented to me, and another sixteen years of effort before my actions took hold. That is a lot of years of uncertainty and discouragement. But, once the climb started, it was a quick rise to what I had been working toward.

I would have preferred a little more visible progress each year; however, as in my case, it is not unusual for long years of frustration to suddenly give way to great leaps forward that could hardly have been imagined just one year earlier.

As long as you are in the fight, good things are possible. Once you give up, you are finished. So, persist. And take heart from this truth:

THE ENTRY-LEVEL CEO

*God often begins to do wonders
after any remaining confidence in our own ability ends.*

The Call

Friends are a special gift. Now, after sixty-plus years of living, I know what a rare gift a true lifelong friend is. I have several lifelong friends. Some went into business, some didn't. Frankly, the ones who settled into jobs with retirements had the easier life.

I tell you this: the ambition to work for yourself can require more from you than you think you have the ability to do. If you can do anything else and be just as happy, do it. *But ...* if you feel a need to be in business for yourself and it won't go away ... well, that constant hunger is your answer. That is probably your intended life path, and your lessons and your blessings are there. It requires much but gives much more.

Don't try to force it, but keep your mind open for a current flowing in the general direction you want to go. The opportunity may not seem like everything you want. But look at it as if you are getting on an "up" elevator. If it will get you closer to the top than your current location, you might want to get on. That's what I mean by stepping into the current.

When I speak with all my friends from earlier years, the ones who chose the path of business have a different level of depth and breadth to them. I'm not saying they are better, but just that their life experiences have made them deeper and broader over the years, as anyone might expect.

There is no one way that fits everyone. We are all here to learn different lessons. We all feel our way forward. In the end, I think it is better when we follow our hearts.

Speaking for myself, I had to do this. Perhaps because of my own weaknesses it was harder for me than most, but I don't regret it. I have been able to provide for my family with less financial restraint. I have grown as a person. I still have character flaws I am working on, but I often tell my wife, "I did a lot wrong in my life, but I did the big things well. The ones that really count in the end. I was a good son, a good father, a good husband, I always did the right things by my customers and employees and suppliers in business, and when the going was hard I just kept going."

I heard once that a young student asked a great composer if he could try composing his own music. The master replied, "No!" The student pointed out that the master himself had composed at a much younger age, to which the master replied, "But I didn't ask anybody for permission. *I had to*!"

Maybe that's the best way to decide this question for yourself.

Despite whatever opinion you may have of me after reading this book, or any of my other books, my business has not made me a rich man as the world measures it, or a famous one. But I have come much closer to the man I was intended to be than I ever could have had I stayed in that police car.

I fought fears much of the way. You will, too; no matter what you do. I took the road less traveled by, as they say. When the demands crushed me, I met my God. When the business blessed me, I was able to fulfill my desire to provide better for my family. Not every decision had to be a dollar issue. Mostly, when I look back and see what I was when the journey began and who I now am, I know this personal growth would not have been possible to me in any other way. *That* is the gift of business, and it is far greater than the money. You don't take the money with you.

A very accomplished friend once told me, "If you are born in a free and prosperous country and you are physically and mentally healthy, that is about as much opportunity as anyone is going to get. The rest is up to you."

I hope, if you feel the relentless urge to be in business for yourself, now that you have read my book, you will answer that call within to become an entry-level CEO.

APPENDIX:
DID THESE IDEAS CROSS YOUR MIND?

In any discussion of how to build and run a successful business—one that can support you for the long haul—a few particular ideas will likely cross your mind. I'd like to comment on those I think might have occurred to you.

Let me begin by saying that you ought not enter into any arrangement to start a business that, if unsuccessful, will put you in a situation from which it will take years to recover. I strongly favor starting small and from scratch, as opposed to investing large sums upfront unless you have experience in that business.

Now, what are some of the money-making opportunities that are commonly considered?

Investing in Real Estate

For the sheer number of men and women who have found a profit in it, real estate is probably second only to business enterprises that provide goods or services.

However, investing in real estate is a field absolutely thick with frenzied people seeking deals. Nevertheless, if you have access to educational courses and possess a passion to succeed at it, I would assume the odds of success are about as favorable here as they are anywhere else.

I would issue one caution concerning real estate: if you decide to look into real estate as a business, do not put a large sum of money into purchasing training courses. If you decide to take a real estate training course—which I recommend you do—*pick only one technique to study.* It is impractical to attempt to learn more than one aspect of real estate investing at a time; no matter what the commissioned salesperson teaching the courses tells you.

Remember, select and pay to learn only one technique. Then, whether the technique suits you or not, do at least one deal successfully in that procedure before paying for other courses. Get your training money back first.

Many hopeful real estate investors become too enthusiastic and end up purchasing expensive educational courses during the glitter show, sometimes spending $10,000 or more, only to realize afterward that real estate is not a quick road to riches but actually hard work in which they do not have a sustainable interest.

In my opinion, it would be wise to spend no more than a few thousand dollars for training until you determine for yourself that you are suited to the business. And absolutely refuse all advice or temptation to assume reckless levels of debt in buying real estate. Progress cautiously as you experience successes.

Most people that make a good portion of their wealth from real estate, already made a good bit of money in business and buy homes to live in, or other real estate investments, that appreciates greatly in value. Time is on their side.

What About Stocks?

I only mention this because I tried and failed at it and I have seen quite a few try it and fail at it. Trading in stocks as an activity to accumulate money is not the same as investing excess capital in the stock market for long-term appreciation. Wealthy men and women may spend a lot of time looking for public companies with bright futures in which to invest, but again, they are long-haul and don't need the money to do anything for them short-term.

As a business enterprise through which to build an independent income, success can only come by active stock speculation, proficiency in which is reserved for men and women possessing a remarkably rare combination of analytical and emotional characteristics. These gifted people do exist, but an "outside the industry" retail trader who has actually made a lasting and dependable income from picking stocks is so rare, I have never met one nor ever known anyone that has met one.

The few people I do know who have accumulated significant amounts of money investing in the stock market made their fortune in their own businesses first and later added to their wealth by investing in stocks. And I know a few who lost a good bit of it that way, too.

However, there will be a very small number of men and women in every generation naturally drawn in this direction, either through the events of their work lives or by inclination, and, for the rare few suited to the task, this would be within the realm of possibility.

If you become enthusiastic after studying some method for profiting from the stock market and decide to attempt it, I would suggest you initially risk no more than twenty percent of your money. If you lose that twenty percent—which is very likely—you can recover. However, if you begin using all your capital and lose it that may take you a long time to recover from.

Not even the most capable stock speculators on Wall Street recommend that you play the game "all in." And margin trading is out of the question. That is strictly reserved for fools.

DID THESE IDEAS CROSS YOUR MIND?

Invent and Market a Product or Create Intellectual Property

Do not be too quick to dismiss this one. Many of the most successful product patents have come from ordinary people and commonplace events.

One version of the story of the invention of the snap button is that a woman created it because fumbling with conventional clothing buttons frustrated her. She patented the "press stud" we all use today and got rich.

Another story tells of a stationer tired of tying an eraser onto the thick pencils in use at the time who then created the attached eraser on the end of a pencil, and it made him wealthy.

Velcro, the popular clothing fastener, was patented by an engineer who looked under a magnifying glass to find out why a particular plant was so hard to get off his clothing and his dog.

If you will keep your eyes open, you too may one day have a profitable idea jump right out at you.

> You must actually be *doing something* in order for good things to happen.

An Italian immigrant opened a small restaurant which made him a living, but that was all. His customers loved his spaghetti and would ask him to make extra so they could take some home to eat later. Only after he noticed how much take-home business he was doing did it occur to him to package some uncooked spaghetti with a can of his sauce and sell it in local stores.

Proud of his Italian heritage and wanting his name to be properly pronounced, he labeled his food product with the phonetic spelling of that name—Chef Boy-ar-dee. He became a multimillionaire.

A man determined to sell his board game teaching the principles of money management was frustrated by the fact that his game was not well understood by its players. So he wrote a booklet to teach the fundamentals of money to help the board game sell. The *booklet* sold like crazy! You may not have heard of his board games, but you probably have heard of the now world-famous, best-selling financial author Robert Kiyosaki and his *Rich Dad* book series.

Another story is told of a young immigrant who arrived in New York from Germany to join his two brothers. Disappointed to find out they were dry goods sellers and not New York millionaires, he learned their craft to survive. When he heard that gold had been discovered in California, he took his savings, bought all the merchandise he could afford, and sailed on a clipper ship around Cape Horn to San Francisco.

Legend has it, he sold almost everything as soon as he arrived, except some rolls of strong tent canvas. He loaded a wagon with the material and set out for the mining fields. One of the first miners he spoke with told him there were no pants available that would stand up to the rigors of mining. Ever alert for an opportunity, this young entrepreneur returned to San Francisco and had pants made of the light canvas called "denim." The pants sold as fast as he could make them, and the Levi Strauss Jean Company was born. Mr. Strauss became fabulously wealthy.

Similar stories are everywhere; life is full of them. The point is this: thinking is important, but it is no substitute for *acting*. It is the man or woman who will stop thinking and start doing who will win out. You have to be *doing something* to succeed. You may not succeed in the thing you are trying to do but acting on that idea may be the very thing that leads you to your true destiny.

> No one knows what he can do till he tries.
> —Publilius Syrus

DID THESE IDEAS CROSS YOUR MIND?

Ideas Require that You Take Action

Just as in the above examples, even if the idea you try for going into business does not work out as you intended, and most of mine did not, if you are pressing forward, good things can happen.

Once you have an idea that will serve a need, if you will begin, success can come in a way other than you expected or the experience can teach lessons vital to your success later.

But nothing is going to change if all you do is talk about needing more money and think about not having enough money and keep complaining to yourself inside your own head about your lack of any way to change things. You must start to think with specific intention to change whatever needs changing. God won't drive a parked car.

George Washington Carver, an African American who was born during the Civil War and did amazing things despite the huge social disadvantages of his times said, "Ninety-nine percent of the failures in the world come from people who have the habit of making excuses." And it is still true.

Mentally stewing in our dissatisfactions, however, can actually be a good thing once we awaken out of that unhappy state. Why? Because, getting "fed-up with it," can provide the fuel to arouse our creative powers. You cannot change something you are willing to accept. "Poor me" thinking won't produce progress; but the moment that the thought, "By God, I am NOT living my entire life like this!" enters your heart … the creative mind *is activated*.

If you want to see improvement in your circumstances, but you see no way right now, the first step is to start using your brain to serve you rather than browbeat you. Use the spare bits of time here and there to envision yourself creating value for others and being paid for it. Don't think about "doing what" exactly. Just see yourself at the next level.

If you can see yourself doing it, if you can believe it, you can create the way to it.

Be willing to ask for guidance in prayer—even if you do not yet normally pray—as this opens you up mentally to ideas and flashes of inspiration from outside yourself. How many people who succeeded later made this revealing statement, "When I heard or saw this or that ... the idea just came to me." Why to them and no one else who may have been standing right beside them? Because their soul, the frequency of thought inside them, was calling for it, seeking it, unconsciously maybe in that moment, but that part of our mind never switches off once it is given a task.

> The best and most beautiful things in the world cannot be seen or even touched—they must be felt with the heart.
> —Helen Keller

Your subconscious mind functions exactly like the servo-mechanism that guides a torpedo to its target. When you give it a goal that has been emotionalized by intense desire and mixed with faith, your mind will begin to seek the most practical means possible to transmute your intangible obsession into a material reality. (Much more on this in *Unchain Your Brain*, the next book in my Common Sense for a Prosperous Life series.) This part of your mind will seize upon and present to you the most practical ideas and means available along your current life path. It is no different than when you forgot a name and tried very hard to remember, but couldn't; then two days later it pops into your mind without effort. That creative part of your mind has been working on providing what you demanded of it, and without you understanding *how*.

Napoleon Hill succinctly summed up this point in his classic bestseller, *Think and Grow Rich*. Mr. Hill wrote that two of the "steps that lead to the habit of persistence" are "a definite purpose backed by a burning desire for its fulfillment" and "a definite plan, expressed in continuous action." The first action to become a future business owner is to have your mind

DID THESE IDEAS CROSS YOUR MIND?

supply you with the idea, and the second is the willingness to test it by action.

If a door opens, or an idea comes—and keeps coming, be willing to step into the current and start moving. Small steps are fine. If you have an idea that truly motivates you, be willing to act. Do not be rash or endanger your ability to care for yourself or your family if things do not work out right away, but be willing to try in sensible ways. If you are on the right track and you will act, God will react.

ABOUT THE AUTHOR

Mark Ashe is the owner of a successful home improvement business in Atlanta. He and his wife of over thirty years have three grown daughters. They enjoy life on their 40-acre farm in the rolling hills of north Georgia, traveling with friends or with their daughters, and great meals shared with close friends. Mark went from being a policeman to debt free and financially independent by his mid-forty's.

Mark writes and speaks with compelling clarity on "common sense for the uncommon life." A wealthy financial adviser has described Mark's writings as "a PhD level course in successful living."

Mark's premise, and the proof of his life, is that an average man or woman can attain surprising success when the desire to do so is strong and the major decisions of life are made with a practical sensibility that his books bring to life through personal examples.

Connect at www.markashe.com

www.ingramcontent.com/pod-product-compliance
Lightning Source LLC
LaVergne TN
LVHW011847060526
838200LV00054B/4216